Practical Care Planning for Personalised Mental Health Care

Edited by

Marjorie Lloyd

 Open University Press

Open University Press
McGraw-Hill Education
McGraw-Hill House
Shoppenhangers Road
Maidenhead
Berkshire
England
SL6 2QL

email: enquiries@openup.co.uk
world wide web: www.openup.co.uk

and Two Penn Plaza, New York, NY 10121-2289, USA

First published 2012

A catalogue record of this book is available from the British Library

ISBN-13: 9780335246267 (pb)
ISBN-10: 0335246265 (pb)
e-ISBN: 9780335246274

Library of Congress Cataloging-in-Publication Data
CIP data has been applied for

Typeset by Aptara Inc., India
Printed in the UK by Bell and Bain Ltd, Glasgow.

Fictitious names of companies, products, people, characters and/or data that may be used
herein (in case studies or in examples) are not intended to represent any real individual,
company, product or event.

MIX
Paper from
responsible sources
FSC www.fsc.org **FSC® C007785**

The **McGraw·Hill** Companies

Practical Care Planning for Personalised Mental Health Care

Praise for this book

"This book is an excellent resource which brings together the essential elements of contemporary mental health practice, providing students with practical and values-based guidance for a range of clinical specialties. The language used throughout is accessible and practice-focused case studies provide stimulus for critical reflection. The principles of recovery and person-centred communication are threaded throughout and guides to care-planning allow the student to navigate through the complexity of balancing personalised care with legal and policy requirements."

Dr Jeanette Hewitt, Lecturer, Swansea University, UK

"This book provides readers with practical examples on how personalised mental healthcare can be achieved in practice. The authors bring to the text their own personal experiences which will benefit learners and enable them to see how theory can be applied in a practical way to resolve complex problems."

Michael Nash, Lecturer, Trinity College Dublin, Ireland

"This book is a useful tool for anyone studying mental health. It gives information about the governmental policies which have shaped mental health practice. The framework of the care plan process is described and useful case studies and examples of care plans from various mental health areas are given in each chapter . . . The reflection exercises and activities set by the authors will help students to understand how to apply the theory to practice."

Deborah Wilson, Mental Health Student Nurse, Sheffield Hallam University, UK

Contents

List of tables

List of figures

Contributors

Alison Owen Traynor is a qualified general nurse and a qualified children's nurse. She is currently a practice educator at Glyndŵr University Wrexham and divides her time between teaching pre- and post-registration nursing students and visiting them in practice. Alison has also worked with looked after children and is therefore very experienced in working within a multidisciplinary team. Alison has worked closely with Child and Adolescent Mental Health Services (CAMHS) in previous roles as a health visitor and specialist nurse for vulnerable children, young people and families. She has a keen interest in collaborative working to improve outcomes for all children.

Brynley Williams is a registered mental health nurse working in older people's mental health care. Brynley has much experience in this field of practice and works as part of a psychiatric liaison team in older people's acute mental health care. His experience contributes to the multidisciplinary inter-professional practice of mental health care for older people and he supports and advises staff in the acute general hospital on providing personalised older people's care.

Carl Benton is a lecturer practitioner (two days a week) in learning disabilities at Birmingham City University and is a member of the Mental Health and Learning Disability Department supporting the pre-registration nursing degree (learning disabilities), specialising in forensic care, risk and mental health. In practice (three days a week) Carl is a senior nurse within the Learning Disability Directorate of Birmingham Community Healthcare Trust. He is a qualified nurse in learning disabilities and mental health and has worked in a variety of settings, both residential and community, for people with complex needs. Carl has publications in the subject of forensic care.

Marie O'Boyle-Duggan is a senior lecturer in learning disabilities at Birmingham City University and is a member of the Mental Health and Learning Disability Department supporting the pre-registration nursing degree (learning disabilities), specialising in behaviour therapy and community nursing leadership prior to her current role within higher education. She is currently developing positive behaviour support, within the curriculum and across the health professions programmes, using live simulation (with patient simulators) as a means of exploring important clinical communication skills and human factors (non-technical skills) required for safe clinical practice and reasonable adjustments. Marie has published this work along with other publications including the involvement of service users with learning disabilities in higher education selection and recruitment.

Marie Yuen is a practice educator and an occupational therapist working in an acute mental health unit. She also teaches undergraduate occupational therapy students in higher education. Marie works as part of a multidisciplinary team in practice ensuring personalised care is available for people suffering from acute mental health problems. Marie also contributes to the planning, teaching and development of higher education programmes of study and enjoys finding innovative ways of helping people to learn about personalised mental health care.

Mark Jukes is a Reader in learning disabilities at Birmingham City University and is a member of the Mental Health and Learning Disability Department supporting the pre-registration nursing degree (learning disabilities). Internationally Mark has recently been instrumental in providing educational support and courses in learning disability in both India and Greece promoting the inclusion agenda for children and adults. Prior to arriving in higher education Mark was a nurse advisor in learning disabilities, and at present supports nurses in a variety of health trusts in practice development. Mark is both a registered mental health and learning disability nurse and practice educator, and has worked within a variety of community and residential supports in both mental health and learning disability nursing services. Mark has published widely in promoting good practice in learning disability nursing.

Marjorie Lloyd is a senior lecturer in mental health nursing at Glyndŵr University Wrexham and has worked previously as a community mental health nurse and a lecturer practitioner. Marjorie contributes to the development of higher educational programmes in mental health care and local therapeutic initiatives in practice. She has published widely in mental health care on empowering practice and care planning in health and social care. Marjorie continues to develop mental health care planning practice believing that it is the basic skills that all mental health practitioners should have and that all service users and carers should be involved in, as equal partners, in developing and delivering effective mental health care.

Matt Phillips is a full-time qualified mental health nurse working with older people in mental health services. Matt has experience of working within the psychiatric liaison multidisciplinary team and developing personalised care planning for older people with mental health problems. Matt is very keen to make people aware of the needs of older people with mental health problems and to reduce the stigma and neglect that has become so evident in the political and media press.

Neil Robdale is an experienced occupational therapist working across the fields of community mental health care and higher education for undergraduate students. Neil is a lecturer practitioner at Glyndŵr University Wrexham and is very involved as a mental health practitioner in the care programme approach for mental health care in the community. Neil is experienced in multidisciplinary and inter-professional working and participates in planning both higher education programmes and the development of community mental health services.

Rowenna Spencer is a mental health nurse manager working with older people who suffer from mental health problems. Rowenna is an active and very experienced practitioner in this field and contributes regularly to the teaching of mental health students, nurses and the wider public on older people's mental health care. Rowenna contributes regularly to developing local and national policy on the teaching and support of health care practitioners across acute health care fields in providing person centred mental health care for older people.

Thomas Currid is an experienced lecturer and practitioner in mental health care at the London South Bank University. Thomas has written and published in the field of mental health care and particularly in primary care and has experience of working within the multidisciplinary team. Thomas has an interest in developing mental health care and in applying policy in primary settings that improves access to psychological therapies (IAPT) for everyone who needs such services.

Introduction

Marjorie Lloyd

Recent enquiries and national reports around health and social care demonstrate a worrying picture of basic care needs being neglected and staff being unsure of their role. At the same time there is pressure upon everyone to avoid waste and to focus upon evidence based practice that can demonstrate improvement in individual and public health. Such surveillance methods may feel very detached from the everyday working practices of individual staff and it may be difficult in such a working environment to feel part of a team who want to provide good quality care. The need for literature and research on providing effective health and social care and planning care well are now even more necessary than before. Recent reports on mental health care provision by the Care Quality Commission (2011) have found that while there is some evidence of good quality care there is room for improvement. They state that:

> The 2011 survey of people who use community mental health services were completed by over 17,000 people aged 16 and over. The results were very similar to those in 2010: overall, 29% of respondents rated the care they had received as excellent, 30% as very good and 20% as good. The vast majority of participants said they were listened to and had trust in their health and social care workers. However, the findings show there is room for improvement, especially in involving people more in some aspects of their care.
>
> (Care Quality Commission 2011: 7)

However, in mental health services we are not alone in trying to improve care provision or planning, and across the whole of the health and social care services in the United Kingdom there is evidence of poor practice which overshadows any attempts to improve services and plan personalised and recovery focused care. The shocking Parliamentary and Health Service Ombudsman's Report *Care and Compassion?* released early in 2011 identifies the problem as not always being about resources but about the individual skills and attitudes of some staff and organizations. In the report featuring the stories of ten older people they found that 'The investigations reveal an attitude – both personal and institutional – which fails to recognise the humanity and individuality of the people concerned and to respond to them with sensitivity, compassion and professionalism' (p. 7).

The King's Fund (Firth Cozens and Cornwell 2009) is a charity that researches healthcare provision and has identified that such lack of involvement in care provision can lead to a lack of compassion, within and for staff and service users. Compassion while difficult to measure they suggest, can be found in the lack of day to day contact with service users and their carers. There appears to be a disturbing trend in such lack of compassion and the consequences of it, which can include a lack of dignity and respect for service users and a lack of support for staff, who then become at risk of compassion fatigue and burnout. This does not mean that staff no longer care, but that in order to survive in the workplace they need to build protective barriers around themselves. This means not getting too involved with service users so that we do not feel their physical or psychological pain and delivering care that fits more within the needs of the organization than the needs of the individual person who requires our care. Struggling with such moral decisions is not a topic of everyday conversation within mental health care but perhaps the time has come that it should be.

Each and every one of us who practise and teach in mental health care should feel comfortable with discussing such difficult topics as relationships, trauma, loss and healing so that we can validate and value the involvement of service users and carers who also have to deal with these issues. Finding a place to become more involved can begin with the care plan that should outline what everyone is prepared to do together to identify and meet the needs of service users and carers. This may then lead to involvement of other practitioners or it may be contained within the one to one therapeutic relationship between practitioner and service user. The most important thing to remember is that we can demonstrate to others how this process has developed and what the eventual goal or outcome will be.

This book is aimed at helping students and practitioners working and studying in the mental health field to explore their care planning practices in more detail. While care planning is a basic feature of all good mental health services it is sometimes neglected as it is seen as simply causing more paperwork. The need to document or record everything that we do as practitioners will always be a professional requirement therefore it is important to make sure that the time spent doing so is effective and efficient. As registered practitioners we are all accountable for our own practice and being able to discuss and explain how we have come to any decision will also develop the morale of all staff in being able to develop their skills confidently. It is therefore necessary in times of austerity and staff migration to develop good care planning skills that will ensure safe and effective practice.

Practical Care Planning for Personalised Mental Health Care will provide plenty of discussion and examples of how we can demonstrate compassion in our everyday work and still demonstrate evidence based practice. The authors of each chapter have experience in that part of practice which focuses upon specific needs of individuals and their carers including young people, older people, people who have learning disabilities and people who need acute or community care. A large proportion of people with mental health care needs only ever have contact with their GP services so we have also included a chapter on primary care mental health needs which are usually addressed by the local GP practice. In taking such a broad view of mental health practice, *Practical Care Planning for Personalised Mental Health Care* demonstrates the subtle boundaries that exist between different service providers and will help the reader to understand the different roles and responsibilities.

While it would be impossible to provide examples of care plans for every diagnosis within mental health care we have focused on some of the main issues or challenges that service users and staff might collaboratively plan care for. In addition we have also acknowledged any influential policy or law that requires us to practise in a certain way. Mental health care is specifically more restricted when it comes to recognising the legal and ethical implications of practice, and if not addressed can lead to oppressive practice, no matter how well-meaning our intentions might be.

Overall this book takes an approach that is different to other theoretical texts in mental health care. It will provide an overview of the main issues that will need to be addressed for effective care to be provided for different groups of people, while at the same time giving examples of how those issues might be addressed. For many people already involved in mental health care this book will act as a critical friend where they can check and provide evidence of the good care that they are already giving or receiving. For those who are new to the field of mental health care it is intended that this book will act as an invisible mentor, guiding people along the path of providing good quality and compassionate care.

It is important that the reader therefore familiarises themselves with the first chapter in this book as it explores the care planning process in more detail. Where possible it has been made specific to the mental health field of practice. The remaining chapters therefore do not need to be read in any particular order, but can be read in relation to the first chapter on planning personalised care. Depending upon where the person or student is in mental health services, the chapter that is most relevant to them will be the obvious choice. However it is advised that all chapters are eventually read so that the reader can differentiate between the roles and responsibilities of all service providers. While it is easy in a book format to neatly package people up into different sections, in reality it is highly unlikely that a person receiving mental health care has not experienced a spectrum of acute, community and primary care services at least. Each chapter therefore will make links with policy and practice in other areas of service provision.

It is not however the intention of this book to provide the most up to date evidence based practice because during the time that it will take to be published there may be more research emerging, particularly in the field of dementia care. Consequently the focus of this book will always be upon personalised care planning first with examples of how evidence based practice can be incorporated. It is therefore the responsibility of the reader to become their own critical friend and to be able to demonstrate the quality of their care planning that is efficient, effective and above all compassionate to the needs of the people that they are caring for.

References

Care Quality Commission (2011) *The State of Health Care and Adult Social Care in England*. London: TSO.

Firth Cozens, J. and Cornwell, J. (2009) *The Point of Care: Enabling Compassionate Care in Acute Hospital Settings*. London: The King's Fund.

Parliamentary and Health Service Ombudsman (2011) *Care and Compassion? Report of the Health Service Ombudsman on Ten Investigations into NHS Healthcare of Older People*. London: TSO.

1 Personalisation and mental health care planning

Marjorie Lloyd

Learning outcomes

After reading this chapter you will be able to:

- Develop an awareness of the law and policy that directs personalised mental health care
- Identify the four main areas of care planning
- Identify the components of a care plan
- Develop an awareness of different models of care planning

Introduction

This chapter will give a brief overview of the care planning process in mental health care. The main policies will be identified in relation to their use in practice. You will be encouraged to reflect upon your own areas of practice and use the rest of this book to develop your care planning skills. This chapter therefore should be read before the other chapters to gather a basic understanding of what is required of people when they are planning personalised mental health care. Terminology and jargon will be kept to a minimum but is required in some places so that an understanding of the different possible meanings can be discussed and reflected upon.

First and foremost this book is about practice and is for those people who work every day, helping other people to recover their independence and maintain a dignified way of living. Each chapter therefore explores the care planning process in a different area of mental health care so that we can learn how to provide effective and efficient mental health care. In this chapter the focus is upon general provision of mental health care and care planning in order to prevent repetition where possible throughout the rest of the chapters and to enable the focus of the book to be on the care planning skills rather than the theory.

Mental health policy in practice

Repper and Perkins (2009) identify many ways in which policy has influenced current mental health practice. National Service Frameworks and strategic policy help guide us towards providing a more personalised and empowering mental health care. Such strategies therefore need to be incorporated into everyday practice if they are to be effective and we should be able to demonstrate that we have done so. Many of the interventions that can be found in personalised care plans have originated from policy and evidence based practice.

One of the most important areas of policy that is becoming more widely accepted across the UK and the world is one that is now more familiarly known as the Recovery Approach (Slade 2009). This approach has developed from listening to service users about what they need to be able to manage their mental illness so that they can continue to live a meaningful life. While there are many authors of the Recovery Approach (Deegan 1996; Davidson et al. 2006; Repper and Perkins 2009), it is generally agreed that it is not a model that must be followed rigidly but more a philosophy for practice. Embedded within this philosophy are some principles that can help us to demonstrate whether our practice is recovery focused or not. Repper and Perkins (2009: 8) state that these include

- **hope** – that a person can regain their confidence and independence;
- **relationships** – that a person can maintain relationships with family and friends as well as professionals;
- **knowledge and understanding** – of what has happened and how it can be treated and managed including dealing with loss;
- **control** – and feeling empowered to do the things that a person needs to do to self-manage their symptoms;
- **opportunity and resources** – to facilitate recovery including housing, money, information and support.

Policy has become an overwhelming part of our everyday practice in health and social care and is difficult and possibly dangerous to ignore. Policy helps us to see the map of care and how what one person does in one area of practice can affect a whole group of people in another (Sainsbury Centre for Mental Health 2009; SCIE 2007). For example risk is an area of mental health care that is very prominent in policy and in law and can sometimes take up all of our time. Policy can provide this guidance so that we do not have to go looking for evidence every time we want to improve our practice (DH 2006). Policy originates from the words police and politics so it could be seen as something that is there to protect both staff and service users as long as we follow the guidance laid out. One important piece of policy influencing mental health care today is the Ten Essential Shared Capabilities (Hope 2004: 3), which can be used to guide our care planning practices.

The ten capabilities help us to become more aware of our day to day practice by

1 **working in partnership** with each other and with service users, carers and other agencies in order to develop an effective care plan;
2 **respecting diversity** by addressing the different needs of individual people and their carers including differences in culture, age, sex, religion

and race. It is not ignorant to discuss diversity with people but it can be harmful if we do not;

3 **practising ethically**, ensuring that every individual has a chance to express their needs and not assuming that we always know best what other people's needs might be;

4 **challenging inequality**; while it may be difficult at times we must always make sure that there is someone to advocate on behalf of the person if they are unable to do so for themselves;

5 **promoting recovery** by encouraging people to make decisions that maintain their hope and optimism in their individual needs being met;

6 **identifying people's needs and strengths** to encourage people along a recovery journey;

7 **providing service user centred care**, working in collaboration at all times to identify and address needs;

8 **making a difference** in helping people to identify and make choices without assuming that they know what is available to them;

9 **promoting safety and positive risk taking** by identifying risks and working together to address them;

10 **ensuring personal development and learning** by taking responsibility for our own learning and providing evidence that our practice is up to date.

The above capabilities include risk but this is put into context with other equally important areas of mental health care practice. This provides us with an holistic or whole way of looking at our practice so that we do not exclude or forget areas that are not so prominent (Lloyd 2010). Challenging inequality may not be the first thing on our minds when we think about our practice but it may be the one thing that is preventing the care plan from being effective. Consider the following scenario.

Case study – Bob

Bob has been off work with depression for six months now. He has many practical skills and is a good driver and operator of machinery. He knows that work can help take his mind off things and you discuss with him how he might be able to return to work. Which of the above capabilities do you think you might use and what will be the main issues for Bob?

After thinking about this case study you may begin to think about what other information or evidence you will need to help people towards their recovery. This will probably include the structure and layout of the care plan that is outlined further below. However in exploring the above basic care plan you may be asking some very important questions of it, such as:

- How do I know that we have identified and addressed all of Bob's needs?
- Who else is likely to become involved in Bob's care?
- Who should I discuss Bob's care plan with?
- How will I know when it has been effective?

Table 1.1 Care plan for Bob

Assessment	Planning	Implementation	Evaluation
Bob suffers from depressed mood and thoughts	Help Bob recover by identify coping skills/ mechanisms	1 Staff to explore treatment options with Bob 2 Review medication and side effects 3 Help Bob develop a supportive network	Weekly until returns to work
Being occupied is a strength for Bob in recovering his independence	Help Bob to find or return to work	1 Help Bob make contact with workplace 2 Discuss risks 3 Discuss strengths 4 Support Bob and employer by providing information with consent from Bob	Weekly then monthly

These questions can be answered by regularly reflecting upon practice and using resources that you have in your area of practice to develop your skills and knowledge. This can be achieved by writing down your thoughts on paper and searching for more evidence to support them; this is known as a reflective account but can also be used to begin a small research study. You might also want to discuss your thoughts with a colleague or your manager. Most professional organizations now have codes of practice or conduct that you can refer to for guidance or support. The important thing to remember in the care planning process is that it is a collaborative communication tool that can be used to ensure that a person gets the best help available. For more information on professional conduct you can visit the Nursing and Midwifery Council (NMC) website which gives a comprehensive account of what is required of registered practitioners in nursing (www.nmc.org) and there are similar guides in medicine, social work, psychology and occupational therapy. We will however consider the ethical implications of personalised mental health care planning later in this chapter.

In order to develop our care planning skills the above questions should have led to an awareness that you may need to find out more. This is where models of practice or theory can help us in searching for new or evidence based information.

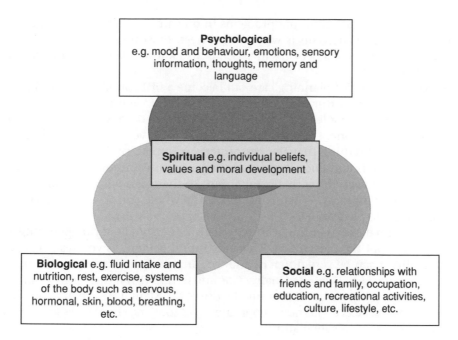

Figure 1.1 Holistic approach to personalised care planning
Source: Adapted from Lloyd (2010)

Figure 1.1 provides a basic outline of where we might need to look. It is based upon an empowerment model identified and discussed in a previous book (Lloyd 2010) that can remind us to develop our skills so that we can demonstrate not only effective services but also compassionate and personalised care. But before you explore Figure 1.1 attempt the activity below.

Activity 1.1 Critical reflection: identifying individual needs

If you have not already been ill think about what your individual or personalised needs might be. How would you obtain help in meeting your needs?

Putting a personalised care plan together

In order to begin writing a care plan we will need to make an assessment of a person's needs. This assessment should cover the four areas in Figure 1.1 in as much detail as necessary. One area is no more important than another to the individual, but they may experience more problems in one area than another.

Likewise they may also find that problems in one area of their life may influence other areas of their life. This is why we will need to explore or assess needs and strengths in all areas of a person's life. This is also known as *holistic* care planning (Lloyd 2010).

In everyday practice planning care can become a little bit like a ritual that you just carry out without thinking too much. However if we want our care plans to be effective for the people that we are helping then we do have to think carefully every time we write one. This is to make sure that we have covered everything and not missed out anything that the person feels is important. To do this properly requires both skills and knowledge. Assessing a person's needs therefore requires that we consider everything that is important to them as a whole person and not just signs and symptoms. When considering the whole person's needs Figure 1.1 will be helpful to refer back to.

Person centred care is at the heart of holistic or personalised care planning and requires us to put the person first. This may sound obvious as you read this book but in reality it can be very different and we can become so busy that the person ends up coming last. The Care Quality Commission (2010) has recently published its first report on its role in monitoring the use of the Mental Health Act and found some interesting facts about how people are cared for. One client gives an example of his involvement in care planning:

> On my previous ward I would often just be invited in for ten minutes at the end of the planning meeting. To wait for two hours then go along to be told that this is what's going to happen to you, this is what we've discussed and this is how it is, I found that pretty degrading. But it does not happen on all wards and certainly not on the ward I am on at the moment.
>
> (Care Quality Commission 2010: 8)

You can also watch Mark talking about his care and other videos on the CQC website (http://www.cqc.org.uk/mentalhealthactannualreport2009-10/videos.cfm).

The skills of care planning

When planning personalised mental health care we therefore need to consider the whole person and their needs alongside the theory or knowledge about mental health care that we already have. We will most probably need to find out more either from the person or from the literature and so the process of care planning becomes circular and in effect never ending (see Figure 1.2). However, the care planning process can also be empowering in that it enables a conversation to take place between the person and the practitioner who is helping them to recover their independence.

You do not need to have a lot of skills to write a care plan but the skills that you do need you have to be very good at. You cannot write a meaningful, effective care plan for someone if you have not paid attention to what they are saying or doing. A

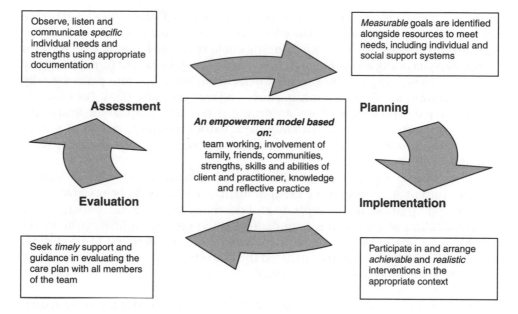

Figure 1.2 An empowerment model of care planning
Source: Adapted from Lloyd (2010)

recent review of communication skills within mental health nursing identified that the skills used when communicating with a person with mental illness are essential to developing a therapeutic relationship (Bowers et al. 2009). The following skills are therefore essential to good care planning in mental health care:

- **communication** – on a one to one basis and in a team, being able to communicate well means that information is shared effectively;
- **listening and attending** – actively so that your body language tells the person that you are genuinely interested in what they have to say;
- **empathy** – in developing a shared understanding of the person's strengths and needs;
- **honesty and truthfulness** – from the beginning so that unrealistic expectations are not formed.

Activity 1.2   Critical appraisal

Stop what you are doing from time to time and think about how you are demonstrating the above skills. Is it something that comes naturally to you or do you have to work at it? What do you need to do to improve your skills and what prevents you from doing this?

Planning care therefore can and should take up a great deal of our time whether we are gathering information from the client and others who know them or if we are monitoring its effectiveness. Care planning could therefore be seen as what we do in our everyday work and should not be viewed as simply a box to be ticked. Many reports of the quality of care provided reflect how good our care plans actually are and inform us of how we can improve our care planning skills. For example in 1997 a man who suffered from autism was detained in hospital for treatment. His carers objected and this led to a huge legal battle and reorganization of mental health care and law now known as the Bournewood gap or Bournewood safeguards (Mental Health Foundation 2005).

The problems identified from Bournewood affect many people who are unable to give consent and required the existing mental health law to be updated and a new law on assessing mental capacity and depriving people of their liberty to be developed. The Mental Health Foundation (2005) provides a briefing paper on the Mental Capacity Act and how it will influence care planning in the future. Some of the main issues to arise included the following, which can now essentially be legally tried as neglect if not addressed:

- the need for appropriate treatment that will alleviate or prevent suffering;
- the need for safety and protection from harm when suffering from mental disturbance;
- the need to communicate needs as individuals and groups when planning care/services;
- the need for carers to become more involved in helping people make choices about their care;
- the need to be more involved in care planning and deciding what individual needs are addressed;
- the need to make choices from options available within health services and the wider community;
- the need to have someone advocate on our behalf when we have been detained under law;
- the need to have our care regularly reviewed and people held to account for their actions.

It is therefore an important and in many cases a legal requirement that we can demonstrate that the person who is in need of our help is at the centre of the care planning process. Care planning helps us to recognise the personal nature of people's needs and identify how we can help them recover their independence. The Department of Health (2009) website for long term conditions states that:

> Personalised care planning is essentially about addressing an individual's full range of needs, taking into account their health, personal, social, economic, educational, mental health, ethnic and cultural background and circumstances. It recognises that there are other issues in addition to medical needs that can impact on a person's total health and well-being.

Case study – Mark

Mark is a 22-year-old student at university. He is studying sociology and would like to work in social sciences and research and travel the world when he obtains his degree. Mark is experiencing frightening thoughts and beliefs that everyone is watching him. He is becoming more and more anxious about going outside and to lectures at the university because he constantly feels in danger. Mark has told no one about how he feels in case it is them who wants to harm him. He is only telling you because he knows you work in the health service and therefore he should be able to trust you. Mark wants you to help him find whoever is going to harm him so that he can continue with his studies. He has a really important exam coming up in the next month and does not want to miss it. Mark is living in student accommodation which is very noisy at night; his parents are both professionals and have busy social lives so he does not get to see them very much. Mark keeps very much to himself and has few friends; he takes his studies very seriously and does not want a university social life that will distract him.

Considering Marks needs how best do you think you can help him? What options or choices do you think Mark has and how will you communicate those to him?

The above exercise may have been difficult to do without a framework to work within. You may have identified a number of areas that Mark will need to think about but how will you document what you have done? Developing a care plan will help you to identify both what Mark thinks his needs are and how they can be addressed. Many care plans follow a similar framework to the one below and you may already be familiar with this layout. It is important to remember that the care plan is an active document constantly requiring updating if it is to be effective. Care planning practice therefore is a skill that we must all learn to develop. There are different frameworks for care planning with different abbreviations but the APIE Framework appears to be the most well recognised (Lloyd 2010). The APIE Framework covers the four areas of care planning practice which are not always given equal weighting when planning care. However if any one of the areas is neglected then the care plan may be destined to fail. The four areas of assessment, planning, intervention and evaluation (APIE) are outlined in Table 1.2.

Care planning using a framework is also known as a systematic approach, which means that each area of planning care is carefully worked through with the service user using good communication skills that were outlined above. Such communication skills also contribute to developing a therapeutic relationship with service users and carers. This relationship is intended to help the person to recover and is therefore different from a friendship or other social relationship. Professional

Table 1.2 Outline of the care planning process

APIE Framework	Area of care planning practice
Assessment	This is an important information gathering process. Communication skills are very important in listening to and checking with the client what they have told you. You may also need to ask other people for information such as friends, carers and other professionals. Whoever you do ask you must always seek the permission of the client to share and gather information about them and act according to your professional code of practice.
Planning	Once a person's needs have been identified we can then begin to think about how they can be addressed. We can do this by discussing realistically how the person might be when they have recovered. It may be important here to discuss short and long term goals so that people have realistic targets to work towards. The case study above identified what Mark eventually wants to achieve (travel the world) and what steps he needs to do that (get his degree).
Implementation	Once the goals have been identified we can then think about how we can achieve them, who will be involved and how much time and effort will be needed. Also how we will measure improvement, which will be important in keeping people motivated in working towards the same goals. If people do not carry out their part at this stage the whole care plan can fail so it is important to be completely honest and realistic with Mark.
Evaluation	This can be a taken for granted part of the care plan but for the same reason is sometimes overlooked. It is important therefore to identify when the care plan will be evaluated and who by. If this is not clearly stated the care plan can become ineffective very quickly.

Source: Adapted from Lloyd (2010).

codes of practice help staff to ensure that the relationship remains therapeutic at all times but there are times when a lack of consideration of the ethics of our practice may affect the relationship developing to its full potential.

Legal and ethical guidance is often needed when assessing a person's ability to make decisions about their care and in planning the right sort of care to meet their individual needs. More recently new parts have been added to mental health law to try and accommodate the needs of individual people who may not want to go to hospital but need substantial forms of support to help them cope with their symptoms. There are now different community mental health teams who might specialise in certain disorders such as substance misuse, or provide a certain kind of help such as home treatment teams. Finding the right kind of help and support is crucial to helping Mark recover quickly and in fostering a supportive relationship between the client and the mental health service providers. Supervised Community Treatment Orders (SCTs or CTOs) have been developed to help people manage their care better but with the support of mental health services under the amended Mental Health Act. The Code of Practice (DH 2008: 220) suggests that:

> The purpose of SCT is to allow suitable patients to be safely treated in the community rather than under detention in hospital, and to provide a way to help prevent relapse and any harm – to the patient or to others – that this might cause. It is intended to help patients to maintain stable mental health outside hospital and to promote recovery.... SCT provides a framework for the management of patient care in the community and gives the responsible clinician the power to recall the patient to hospital for treatment if necessary.

It goes on to suggest that personalised care planning must be in place in order for supervised community treatment orders to be successful:

> Good care planning, in line with the Care Programme Approach (CPA) (or its equivalent) will be essential to the success of SCT. A care co-ordinator will need to be identified. This is likely to be a different person from the responsible clinician, but need not be.

The care plan should be prepared in the light of consultation with the patient and (subject to the normal considerations of patient confidentiality):

- the nearest relative;
- any carers;
- anyone with authority under the Mental Capacity Act 2005 (MCA) to act on the patient's behalf;
- the multi-disciplinary team involved in the patient's care; and
- the patient's GP (if there is one). It is important that the patient's GP should be aware that the patient is to go onto SCT. A patient who does not have a GP should be encouraged and helped to register with a practice.

(DH 2008: 223)

The Mental Health Act (1983) was amended in 2007 following a lengthy consultation about changes that needed to be made after tragic events had taken place in the community where failure to continue treatment had occurred for some clients. Practices were also called into question that were too restrictive or were harmful to the physical health of clients and did not comply with The Human Rights Act of 1998. The Community Care Act of 1990 was considered to have failed people in the care of mental health services and so radical changes were made which included

- the development of supervised community treatment orders as outlined above;
- the development of law to assess and protect the needs of carers in 2000 and 2004;

- the development of the Mental Capacity Act in 2005;
- the development of Deprivation of Liberty Safeguards (DOLs) in 2009;
- the development of the Equality Act 2010;
- a five yearly report on the homicides and suicides in mental health services from 2001;
- national guidance on treatments including prescribing practices from NICE and SCIE (National Institute for Clinical Excellence and the Social Care Institute for Excellence).

All of the above were intended to improve practice and develop the skills of practitioners when planning care in collaboration with individual clients (King's Fund 2008). However the Mental Health Act of 1983 remains in place with the amendments added as outlined in Table 1.3.

In addition, some changes to the definition of a mental disorder were made because some people had been refused treatment even when they asked for it, because they were assessed as not having a mental illness that was treatable. Some of those people had gone on to commit fatal acts after failing to get help from the mental health services. The Department of Health (2008) Code of Practice therefore clearly lays out what the new definition means on page 19:

Definition of mental disorder
Mental disorder is defined for the purposes of the Act as 'any disorder or disability of the mind'. Relevant professionals should determine whether a patient has a disorder or disability of the mind in accordance with good clinical practice and accepted standards of what constitutes such a disorder or disability.

Clinically recognised conditions which could fall within the Act's definition of mental disorder

- affective disorders, such as depression and bipolar disorder
- schizophrenia and delusional disorders
- neurotic, stress-related and somatoform disorders, such as anxiety, phobic disorders, obsessive compulsive disorders, post-traumatic stress disorder and hypochondriacal disorders
- organic mental disorders such as dementia and delirium (however caused)
- personality and behavioural changes caused by brain injury or damage (however acquired)
- personality disorders
- mental and behavioural disorders caused by psychoactive sub-stance use (but see paragraphs 3.8–3.12 Mental Health Act Code of Practice)
- eating disorders, non-organic sleep disorders and non-organic sexual disorders

Table 1.3 Brief overview of the main sections of the Mental Health Act (1983 amended 2007)

Section of the Act	Practice	Appeals	2007 Amendments
Section 2 Admission to hospital for Assessment	Can be detained in hospital for up to 28 days for assessment – not renewable Requires two doctors and one Approved Mental Health Practitioner (AMHP)	Can appeal against the decision in writing	Definition of mental illness changed to cover all disorders – Approved Social Worker (ASW) replaced with Approved Mental Health Practitioner (AMHP)
Section 3 Admission to hospital for treatment	Can be detained in hospital for up to six months for treatment – renewable Requires two doctors and one Approved Mental Health Practitioner (AMHP)	Can appeal in writing against decision Second Opinion Approved Doctor (SOAD) may be called for treatment decisions after three months	Can now be transferred quickly to a CTO under Section 117 below SOAD required mandatory for some treatments e.g. electroconvulsive therapy (ECT)
Section 4 Admission to hospital for emergency assessment	Can be detained in hospital for up to 72 hours – not renewable Requires one doctor and one Approved Mental Health Practitioner (AMHP)	Cannot appeal and should only be used in an emergency	
Section 5.2 Detain while already in hospital for assessment	Can be detained in hospital by one doctor for up to 72 hours or transferred to another section	Cannot appeal and should only be used in an emergency	
Section 5.4 Detain while already in hospital for assessment	Can be detained in hospital by one registered mental health or learning disability nurse for up to six hours or transferred to another section	Cannot appeal and should only be used in an emergency	
Section 117 Right to aftercare following discharge from hospital	Right to aftercare if previously been detained on a Section 3 only	Not to be used for detaining a client but to ensure access to services is given as a priority – no appeal necessary	Amendments made to this section to accommodate Supervised Community Treatment Orders (SCTs or CTOs)

- learning disabilities (but see paragraphs 3.13–3.15)
- autistic spectrum disorders (including Asperger's syndrome) (but see paragraphs 3.16–3.17)
- behavioural and emotional disorders of children and adolescents

(Note: this list is not exhaustive.)

Ethical considerations when planning personalised mental health care

It is important to keep Mark's wishes in mind at all times and in mental health care and law the person's best interests must always be upheld. However, when making decisions with a person about their care needs, ethical conflict can arise. It is important to recognise and address such ethical conflict so that the appropriate interventions can be planned and put into place as soon as possible. Considering Mark's case study above there are a number of ethical conflict issues that can arise and which, if not addressed, may sabotage the whole care planning process. For example:

- Mark may not think he has any symptoms as such but is aware that he is feeling frightened. The role of the person helping him is therefore to help him identify what he needs to do to feel less frightened.
- Mark is a very independent person and considers his ability to study alone a strength. In collaboration with Mark the person helping him plan his care needs will need to take this into account and not expect Mark to join lots of social groups.
- Mark is not taking any medication at present and may not understand why he should be taking medication for what he thinks is other people's behaviour. Mark may need information on how medication can help him cope with his feelings.
- Mark is isolating himself and does not have a support network to help him cope in an emergency. Helping Mark to identify a support network will also help him to cope with distressing feelings.

It is important to identify the main areas that Mark needs help with and there could be many, but at the moment he is asking for help with how he is feeling. It would not be appropriate to begin formal admission under the Mental Health Act until all other avenues have been tried. A care plan will then document what you have discussed and how you intend to help Mark, which can also be shared with other people who will be involved, with consent from Mark. Current mental health law requires that all attempts are made to involve people in their care plan and that force, in the form of detention, should only be used as a last resort or when the risk becomes too great to a person's mental wellbeing. For further information about interpreting mental health law in practice see the Codes of Practice for the Mental Health Act 1983 (amended 2007) and the Mental Capacity

Act 2005 but these may vary in different countries and governments. The Code of Practice for the Mental Health Act for England (Department of Health 2008; and adapted elsewhere) is based upon five main guiding principles which are:

1   **Purpose principle** Mental health law should only be used to enable the safety of individuals and others, to reduce distress and to support mental wellbeing and recovery.

2   **Least restriction principle** Any actions taken without the consent of the person should keep to a minimum the restrictions made upon the person.

3   **Respect principle** When taking actions with and for a person their holistic and diverse needs should be respected at all times, including their biopsychosocial and spiritual needs.

4   **Participation principle** People should be involved in their care plan at all times and stages and carers should be encouraged to participate where possible and agreed by the client.

5   **Effectiveness, efficiency and equity principle** All resources available should be used to ensure that the person receives the most appropriate help at the right time in order to ensure an effective care package is in place.

While the above are simply principles and are therefore not law in their own right, they can help as a guide when planning personalised mental health care. The care plan for Mark (see Table 1.4) therefore takes into account the above principles and his holistic care needs and focuses upon promoting mental health recovery.

Writing SMART care plans

An effective care plan is one that can be read by any member of the healthcare team and acted upon without seeking further clarification. If the care plan is too elaborate or simple it may obscure vital information and be less efficient in meeting the goals that have been collaboratively created between the care coordinator and client. An effective personalised care plan is therefore **SMART**, which means: **S**pecific assessment of needs is identified, **M**easurable goals of planning so that we know when it has been achieved, **A**chievable goals and interventions that are **R**eliable and not dependent upon long waiting lists for further services and **T**imely interventions and evaluations to make sure everyone feels safe and comfortable with the current care plan. (See Lloyd 2010 for more indepth discussion of care planning.)

Mark's care plan is basic but can be found in the evidence discussed previously. It is important to know where the evidence for the care plan comes from and that it is not something that has been written to comply with a practice policy. The professional knowledge and support of the care coordinator is essential in helping people to access the most effective and efficient services and support as soon as possible in order to minimise risk and promote safety (DH 2008). In Mark's care

Table 1.4 Care plan for Mark

Assessment	Planning	Implementation	Evaluation
1 Mark feels afraid that people are going to harm him	To reduce feelings of harm and help Mark cope with his feelings	1 Arrange for Mark to speak with a doctor about medication and attend any associated clinics 2 Care coordinator to discuss with Mark other ways in which he can cope with his feelings	Weekly follow up initially by named care coordinator Review weekly
2 Mark is an independent person and can usually manage his daily activities very effectively	To help Mark create an advanced directive/ statement and crisis plan	1 Weekly meetings with care coordinator to make future management plans (Mondays free from lectures)	Evaluate and review weekly
3 Mark has very little support to help him cope with how he is feeling	Help Mark identify a support network of people he can trust to help him in a crisis	1 As part of developing the crisis plan each week make a list of contact names and numbers available 2 Ensure Mark has access to a phone 3 Help Mark access support groups and services of his choice either with a peer or health/social care support worker	Review weekly Review daily in first week Review monthly

plan you can see that his needs were addressed to help him cope with his feelings so that he can feel safe again and to provide enough support so that the risk of him feeling this way for much longer is minimised. Mental health recovery is also incorporated in ensuring that Mark develops a stronger support network around him and that he can identify and use his strengths to help him do this. The role of the care coordinator is to provide support, advice and guidance during this recovery process.

Adopting a recovery focused approach to personalised mental health care

In completing this chapter, which provides an overview of the personalised care planning process, it is worth remembering that recovery should influence all personalised care plans if they are to be recovery focused. The National Institute for Mental Health in England (2005: 3) produced a *Guiding Statement on Recovery* which included the following principles:

Principle I The user of services decides if and when to begin the recovery process and directs it; therefore, service user direction is essential throughout the process.

Principle II The mental health system must be aware of its tendency to promote service user dependency. Users of service need to be aware of the negative impact of co-dependency.

Principle III Users of service are able to recover more quickly when their:

- Hope is encouraged, enhanced and/or maintained
- Life roles with respect to work and meaningful activities are defined
- Spirituality is considered
- Culture is understood
- Educational needs as well as those of families/significant others are identified
- Socialisation needs are identified
- They are supported to achieve their goals.

Principle IV Individual differences are considered and valued across the life span.

Principle V Recovery from mental illness is most effective when a holistic approach is considered; this includes psychological, emotional, spiritual, physical and social needs.

Principle VI In order to reflect current 'best practices' there is a need for an integrated approach to treatment and care that includes medical/

biological, psychological, social and values-based approaches. A recovery approach embraces all of these.

Principle VII Clinicians' and practitioners' initial emphasis on 'hope' and the ability to develop trusting relationships influence the recovery of users of services.

Principle VIII Clinicians and practitioners should operate from a strengths/assets model.

Principle IX Users of service with the support of clinicians, practitioners and other supporters should develop a recovery management or wellness recovery action plan. This plan focuses on wellness, the treatments and supports that will facilitate recovery, and the resources that will support the recovery process.

Principle X Involvement of a person's family, partner and friends may enhance the recovery process. The user of service should define whom they wish to involve.

Principle XI Mental health services are most effective when delivery is within the context of the service user's locality and cultural context.

Principle XII Community involvement as defined by the user of service is central to the recovery process.

Activity 1.3   Critical reflection on the principles of recovery

Does your practice include all of the principles above? If not how could you improve it? Try writing a care plan with the above principles as a guide.

The above principles could be applied to Mark's care plan above in order to check that recovery focused interventions are in place. In helping Mark manage his symptoms we are also helping him to develop personalised self-management skills for the future. The care plan could then be developed into a crisis plan indicating for Mark how he would like to be helped in the future and/or an advanced statement which provides information on what Mark would not like to happen. Mark may also wish to develop a wellness recovery action plan (WRAP) which will be based upon his strengths and skills and not necessarily upon his symptoms. For more information on WRAP go to the website of its founder Mary Ellen Copeland (http://www.mentalhealthrecovery.com/) where information on the process and training can be found. You can also visit the Scottish Recovery Network for more information on recovery and WRAP training (http://www.scottishrecovery.net/). In all our attempts to develop evidence based practice it is important to remember that we are working with people first and foremost. Patricia Deegan (1996), a service user herself, reminds us that each person we meet in our personal and professional life has a heart but it is a wise practitioner who remembers that it is a human heart not a mechanical one:

> Wisdom would seek the form or essence of the heart. In wisdom we would see that the anatomical heart, which we have given our students to study, is nobody's heart. It is a heart that could belong to anybody and therefore it belongs to nobody. Wisdom would have us understand that there is another heart. There is a heart that we know about long before we are taught that the heart is a pump. I am speaking here of the heart that can break; the heart that grows weary; the hardened heart; the heartless one; the cold heart; the heart that aches; the heart that stands still; the heart that leaps with joy; and the one who has lost heart. Wisdom demands that we teach students of the human sciences about the essence of this heart. The human heart.
>
> (Deegan 1996: 91)

Conclusion

The above care plan and overview of mental health services requires a lot of information to be understood and practised if we are going provide personalised and recovery focused mental health care. Personalised care planning however is largely an ethical endeavour in that we are all attempting to keep the person's best interests at the centre of the care planning process. Sometimes the management of risk and other resources may make practitioners feel like we are being prevented from carrying out our job to the best of our ability. It is very important in that case that we ensure the best services are available for the people who need them and that we all work in a collaborative and recovery focused way. Developing our practice towards a more recovery focused person centred approach will enable us to ensure that the person remains at the centre of the care planning process.

References

Bowers, L., Brennan, G., Winship, G. and Theodoridou, C. (2009) *Talking with Acutely Psychotic Patients: Communication Skills for Nurses and Others Spending Time with People who are Very Mentally Ill*. London: City University.

Care Quality Commission (2010) *Monitoring the Use of the Mental Health Act in 2009/10*. London: Care Quality Commission.

Davidson, L., Chinman, M., Sells, D. and Rowe, M. (2006) Peer support among adults with serious mental illness: a report from the field. *Schizophrenia Bulletin*, 32(3): 443–50.

Deegan, P. (1996) Recovery as a journey of the heart. *Psychiatric Rehabilitation Journal*, 19(3): 91–7 (http://www.bu.edu/cpr/repository/articles/pdf/deegan1996.pdf) (accessed 5 February 2012).

DH (Department of Health) (2006) *From Values to Action: The Chief Nursing Officer's Review of Mental Health Nursing. Summary*. London: TSO.

DH (2008) *Code of Practice: The Mental Health Act 1983*. London: TSO (http://www.dh.gov.uk/prod_consum_dh/groups/dh_digitalassets/@dh/@en/documents/digitalasset/dh_087073.pdf) (accessed 5 February 2012).

DH (2009) *Care Planning: Long Term Conditions*. London: TSO (http://www.dh.gov.uk/en/Healthcare/Longtermconditions/DH_093359) (accessed 5 February 2012).

Hope, R. (2004) *The Ten Essential Shared Capabilities: A Framework for the Whole Mental Health Workforce*. London: HMSO.

King's Fund (2008) *Briefing: Mental Health Act 2007*. London: The King's Fund.

Lloyd, M. (2010) *A Practical Guide to Care Planning in Health and Social Care*. Maidenhead: Open University Press.

Mental Health Foundation (2005) *Executive Briefing: The Mental Capacity Act*. London: Mental Health Foundation.

National Institute for Mental Health in England (2005) *Guiding Statement on Recovery*. London: Department of Health.

Repper, J. and Perkins, R. (2009) Recovery and social inclusion. In C. Brooker and J. Repper (eds) *Mental Health: From Policy to Practice*. Oxford: Elsevier, pp. 1–13.

Sainsbury Centre for Mental Health (2009) *Implementing Recovery: A New Framework for Organizational Change*. London: Sainsbury Centre for Mental Health.

SCIE (2007) *A Common Purpose: Recovery in Future Mental Health Services*. London: Social Care Institute for Excellence.

Slade, M. (2009) *100 Ways to Support Recovery: A Guide for Mental Health Professionals*. London: Rethink (http://www.sswahs.nsw.gov.au/mhealth/content/pdf/100_ways_to_support_recovery.pdf) (accessed 5 February 2012).

Useful websites

Care Quality Commission http://www.cqc.org.uk/

2 Mental health in primary care

Thomas J. Currid

Learning outcomes

After reading this chapter you will be able to

- Demonstrate an understanding of the evolving role, policy and function of primary care mental health services
- Discuss patient profiles and challenges presented in primary care mental health services
- Use conceptualization frameworks that provide greater insights to patients' distress
- Formulate a care plan takes account of contemporary mental health practice

Introduction

Primary care services are those that provide facilities at the first point of contact in health care systems. Unlike secondary or specialist services, you do not need to be refered by another professional; rather, they may operate on a self-referral basis. Typical services include general practitioners (GPs), dentists, health promotion services, walk in centres, and telephone services like NHS Direct. As the range of facilities offered in primary care is diverse along with the numbers of professionals, it further increases the likelihood of coming in contact with varying forms of mental illness. Ninety per cent of mental health problems are cared for solely in primary care settings (AMRC 2009) and are now implicated in one in four primary care consultations. Mental health consultations are second only to those with respiratory infections (McCormick et al. 1995). Considering mental health is an inextricable dimension of holistic health, it is hardly surprising that mental illness is common in primary care. Presentations may vary from temporary reactions to life events such as grief or loss to more severe forms of co-occurring complex and disabling conditions. To illustrate this, we'll meet Afaf.

Case study – Afaf

Afaf is a 26-year-old woman who came to live in Birmingham from Pakistan at the age of 10. Following some school difficulties at the age of 12, Afaf was diagnosed with a mild learning disability. During her teenage years, Afaf's parents became very protective and controlling resulting in many arguments between them. Her parents report that she became uncontrollable and had little respect for their customs or traditions. At the age of 19, Afaf left home to live with her uncle in London. Her uncle had not agreed with this, and after a couple of weeks following what her uncle describes as disrespectful behaviour, Afaf was asked to leave. She managed to get several part time jobs and secure a tenancy in a local authority flat. Afaf became friendly with a retired Irish woman: Mrs O'Bama, whom she found to be very supportive and kind. Later, Afaf stopped visiting her as she considered Mrs O'Bama to be patronizing, using phrases such as 'good girl' or 'poor thing'. Afaf recalls a time when she was having difficulties with a shop keeper and Mrs O'Bama came to her defence saying he shouldn't speak to Afaf like that because she is 'mentally handicapped'.

Recently, Afaf gave birth to a baby girl called Elizabeth. During her pregnancy, Afaf developed gestational diabetes and frequently visited her GP voicing concerns about her pregnancy. These centred on giving birth and the fear of pain and dying in labour. She was referred to social services for extra support. However, Afaf did not engage and suspected that social services was there to monitor whether or not she was capable of parenthood. She commenced antenatal classes but did not continue as she said that they did not help because the midwife asked her on several occasions to let others speak. Also, she said she did not 'connect' with the other expectant mothers because they were 'horrible bitches' who laughed at her and called her a 'nutter'. Another example she gave was that when the group went for coffee after antenatal classes, they would not tell her which coffee shop that they were going to so as to prevent her from joining them. To help cope with many of these distressing issues, Afaf began to drink a bottle of wine each night.

Following the premature birth of her baby, the midwife visited her frequently along with her health visitor. They both voiced concerns about her welfare, her drinking and angry behaviour. After screening, she was considered to have moderate levels of anxiety and severe depression. They referred her to the learning disabilities community team and asked the psychiatrist to carry out a domiciliary visit. Afaf became very angry about this and threatened to go away where services could not contact her. She accused both the midwife and health visitor of treating her as if she was 'mad' when all she needed was a few nights of good sleep.

Planning holistic care

As in Afaf's case, there are a number of predisposing and precipitating factors that can contribute to experiences of distress. When planning care, it is imperative to take account of historic and recent bio-psychosocial events.

George Engel (1977) proposed the bio-psychosocial model which postulates that in order to treat patients effectively and compassionately, one must take account of the simultaneous personal dynamics of the biological, psychological and sociological aspects. Though this approach to care may seem obvious now, at that time, the biomedical model prevailed in industrialised societies and had done so since the beginning of the twentieth century. Engel did not accept the reductionist view that phenomena arise from a primary principle (such as disordered somatic processes) independent of other variables, but rather that illness or distress was an interacting amalgam of somatic and psychosocial factors (Engel 1977). As Borrell-Carrió et al. (2004) assert, Engel did not only champion his ideas as a scientific proposal, but also as a fundamental ideology that challenged the dehumanization of medicine and disempowerment of patients. Since then, this accepted model has been adopted in most health and social care professional groups as a means of understanding and treating illness in an individualised manner.

Activity 2.1   Critical reflection: getting started

It may be helpful to put yourself in Afaf's shoes for this reflection. What predisposing issues can you identify that may be contributing to this current state? Afaf developed gestational diabetes. Often when we have poor health, we may feel particularly vulnerable. Might this account for some of the behaviours such as frequent attendance at the GP? Draw a pie chart and write biological, psychological and social factors that may contribute to this presentation. Now see if you can identify how one may be impacting on the other or whether one may be maintaining the other. For example, alcohol is a known depressant, therefore it may be contributing to Afaf's mood. Tiredness can make you agitated and may lead to bouts of hostility.

Holism in practice

Despite the acceptance of this more holistic approach, there is still evidence where service provision and those responsible for delivering care may not be adequately addressing or considering the holistic nature of distress and its accompanying needs. Both policy and research continue to identify how people with mental health issues experience adversities and inequalities that require immediate attention. The Coalition Government's recent mental health strategy

No Health Without Mental Health (DH 2011b: 8) acknowledges that improvements have been made in mental health services; however it also recognises that: 'too often, commissioning of mental health services has not received the attention at senior level that it requires. The focus has been on specifying what mental health providers should do, rather than on improving the quality of mental health commissioning'. In short, those who have been privileged with brokering services for us all have failed to look at their own practice of ascertaining what to commission, but instead have invested heavily in telling front line services (who have greater experience and knowledge of what patients want) what to do.

Similarly from a care perspective, the Care Quality Commission (2011) found that in the last year over a third of mental health respondents said that they had not received enough support with physical health care needs. Other reports also identify groups where their needs go unmet.

Michael (2008) identified how people with learning disabilities often have unmet needs brought about by issues such as 'diagnostic overshadowing' where staff attribute symptoms to their learning disability rather than valuing and seeing people with a learning disability as having needs equal to the general population. While this approach undermines dignity, individualism and respect, it also identifies how care planning activities are not being undertaken in line with best practice. Within the field of child and adolescent mental health, the Office of the Children's Commissioner (2007) identified the lack of information and involvement in care planning for those admitted onto adult acute wards. In the respondents' narratives offered, care was typified as supportive, but often without involvement in decisions, and as lacking information on risks and treatment.

Though many variables may contribute in providing less than optimum care, care planning at both macro and micro levels has a pivotal role in improving services. While we all have a role to play in improving and delivering responsive quality services, there are key areas that need immediate attention. These include commissioning services based on what patients need, provision of biopsychosocial care that reflects a Recovery based philosophy and appreciates the patient's story and expertise (Barker 2003), and finally a knowledgeable workforce who have the skills, competence and leadership qualities to meet with the requirements of an ever evolving healthcare system.

Using a 'bottom up' approach, we will see later in the chapter how staff who directly care for patients are in a strong position to perpetuate proficiency by influencing and delivering patient care that is empowering, meaningful and effective. To do so requires them to take a holistic, patient centred, evidence based approach that reflects partnership working both in the conceptualization and treatment of the patient's experience of distress. Using a Recovery framework in context to a care plan template, these 'best practice' features will be explored later following an overview of mental health policy and key issues in primary care. However before doing so, it may be helpful to reflect on the above paragraphs in the context of your own experience and to identify how the best practice features identified above may impact on services and the care that you provide.

Activity 2.2   Critical reflection: creating awareness

Based on your reading so far, along with your experience of help seeking from health and social care services, consider whether you felt your need was set in context to a bio-psychosocial framework. As most people reading this book will have visited their GP, you may want to use this experience for your reflection. Questions that may help you to do this include:

1   Did the care provider take a holistic approach to your presenting complaint or did the presenting complaint 'overshadow' other segments of
the holistic framework?
2   Did you realise the holistic nature of your health need or did you view it
within a uni-dimensional concept?
3   In answer to questions 1 and 2, what may be the distal factors that
influenced the care provider and your view? And finally, in relation to
your own knowledge, skills and values, what are the areas that you
consider you need to improve upon?

Issues and challenges

Thus far, it is evident that a number of challenges are beginning to present. Whether these pertain to the complexities of issues that present in primary care, unmet needs not being addressed or the requirement of continuous improvement and quality of service, mental health primary care services continue to pose a number of challenges. Identifying this, the King's Fund (2011) state that: 'In spite of the high profile given to mental health by recent governments, certain challenges have proven difficult to address. Social outcomes for people with mental health problems remain poor, profound inequalities exist, provision of mental health support in primary care is patchy, and waiting times for psychological therapies can still be high'.

Though a plethora of factors may contribute to challenges, at this stage it may be pertinent to look at attitudes and discriminatory issues that may have impacted on service provision.

Stigma and legislation

From a historical context, public negative attitudes to mental illness have always been around and from a service provision perspective, mental health and learning disabilities have been considered as the 'Cinderella services' of health care provision. As Byrne (2000) purports, despite centuries of learning, mental illness is still seen as a sign of weakness, discredit and shame that has many adverse experiences for the individual. These include isolation, secrecy, discrimination and social exclusion. It does not stop with the individual, since family members and friends may also experience 'courtesy stigma' (Goffman 1963) by the mere fact of being associated with the mentally ill. Though stigma may be understood in terms of attitude brought about by not having sufficient knowledge of mental illness, it is not just a feature of public attitude. Staff working in the field of mental health also may be stigmatised. Halter (2008) in her study of 'Perceived characteristics of psychiatric nurses: stigma by association', found that mental health nurses are viewed negatively by nurses in other specialities. Findings suggest that mental health nurses are perceived as weak, incompetent, idle, and unskilled, characteristics that mirror public attitude to the mentally ill (Byrne 2000).

Other literature would support these contentions that the stigma of mental illness is evident at various levels in service provision. The Royal College of Psychiatrists (2008) in its 'fair deal' manifesto highlights how stigma can occur within the health service at both individual and institutional level. They argue that stigma adversely affects policy development unfairly, usually through omission of relevant mental health issues and policies. They call on the NHS to 'get its own house in order'. Yet, the Human Rights Act (HRA) (1998) legally protects those with mental illness. Examples include the following: Article 3 – Prohibition of Torture states that: No one shall be subjected to torture or to inhuman or degrading treatment or punishment; Article 8 – Right to respect for private and family life (1) states that: Everyone has the right to respect for his private and family life, his home and his correspondence; Article 14 – Prohibition of discrimination states that: The enjoyment of the rights and freedoms set forth in this Convention shall be secured without discrimination on any ground such as sex, race, colour, language, religion, political or other opinion, national or social origin, association with a national minority, property, birth or other status.

Implementing the HRA using a 'bottom up' approach, the Royal College of Psychiatrists has introduced a framework that avoids the need for technical knowledge of the Act but provides a core values process that can be used to adhere and protect patients in clinical practice. The FREDA (fairness, respect, equality, dignity, and autonomy) principles set out below, roughly equate to various articles of the HRA (Curtice et al. 2010: 1):

- Fairness – Article 6 = right to a fair trial
- Respect – Article 8 = right to private and family life
- Equality – Article 14 = prohibition of discrimination
- Dignity – Article 3 = freedom from torture, inhuman and degrading treatment
- Autonomy – Article 8

Another Act that protects the rights of people with mental illness is the Equality Act (2010). The Act sets out to ensure there is equality and fairness for people who may have a disability, thus preventing discrimination. It also provides rights for people who have an association with a disabled person to be protected against harassment or discrimination.

Activity 2.3   Critical reflection: embracing fundamental values

Using Afaf's case and informed by paragraphs pertaining to negative attitudes and prejudice, identify whether she may have experienced this. Now using your own life experience to date, consider whether you have witnessed prejudice. If so, what was the setting? Was it from the public or was it from professionals? How do you think that you could implement anti-discriminatory practice and policy within care plans? Consider what are your own value belief systems. Do they match those of FREDA?

Primary care mental health policy

Any government healthcare policy will bring with it many changes that will have an impact on the organization of care at various levels. Of course, change will also have an impact on other areas including patients, relatives, you, economic or education. However in this section we will specifically explore how mental health policy has impacted on patients, professionals and practice in an attempt to improve quality delivery and as a means of perpetuating proficiency. As an aid to understanding this, it may be helpful to think of it as an interacting and interdependent five systems model (see Figure 2.1).

Since the 1990s a number of changes have taken place in mental health services that have had a direct impact on mental health service provision in primary care. It may be pertinent at this stage to remember that up until then, mental illness carried quite a large element of stigma. In 1990, the National Health Service and Community Care Act was introduced. In essence, the Act required local authorities (social services) and health authorities to work together to provide care for patients in the community. This was the beginning of an internal market system in health care where providers competed with one another to provide services. Simultaneously, many of the large psychiatric hospitals were closing and discharging patients back into community settings. To assist with the introduction of the National Health Service and Community Care Act (1990), in 1991, the Care Programme Approach was introduced. This set requirements for health authorities to ensure that each person with severe mental illness had a care plan in place that met with their needs. To strengthen policy initiatives arising from the aforementioned documents, and in an attempt to 'iron out' some of the challenges that were arising (these include integrating service provision to provide seamless care, addressing some of the issues that arose from high profile homicides), in 1995, *Building Bridges: A Guide to Arrangements for Inter-agency Working for the Care and Protection of Severely Mentally Ill People* (DH 1995) was introduced. Among other content, this document asserted that care needs to be seamless and that efforts should focus on those with severe and enduring mental illness. At the time, an attempt to define severe mental illness was made. This centred on Diagnosis, Disability, Duration, Safety and Informal or

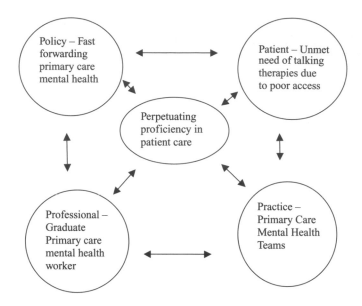

Figure 2.1 An example of interacting and interdependence model

Formal care (sectioned or not). To distinguish between groups of patients who may have differing needs, the term 'common mental health problems' was used to define those with non-psychotic illnesses who had shorter episodes of need and experienced less disability. However, while services for those with a serious mental illness were high on the agenda at the time, there was less focus on those with common mental health problems. Despite adequate preparation, primary care practitioners were expected to manage and treat those that fell into this category.

As is beginning to emerge, relating policy to practice can sometimes be difficult and complex (Onyett 2003). In part this may be due to the generalist background of the staff working in primary care. Armstrong (2001) asserts most primary care workers have little or no formal training in psychiatry beyond their initial training. Building on these issues, Currid (2003) asserts that staff in the field of primary care often do not recognise mental health difficulties and may not have the skills or competence needed to provide a quality user led service.

In 1999, following the then Secretary for Health Frank Dobson's statement that 'community care has failed' (Burns and Priebe 1999), the National Service Framework for mental health: modern standards and service models (NSFMH) was introduced. Unlike previous mental health policies which focused mainly on secondary care services, standards two and three of the NSFMH made specific reference to primary care. Standard two of the framework stated that: any service user who contacts their primary health care team with a common mental health problem should:

- have their mental health needs identified and assessed, be offered effective treatments, including referral to specialist services for further assessment, treatment and care if they require it.

Standard three stated that any individual with a common mental health problem should:

- be able to make contact round the clock with the local services necessary to meet their needs and receive adequate care;
- be able to use NHS Direct, as it develops, for first-level advice and referral on to specialist helplines or to local services.

Though a definition of common mental health problems was not offered, the framework did allude to depression, eating disorders and anxiety as being the most common. To operationalise this, the NHS Plan of 2000 (DH 2000) proposed the introduction of 1000 new graduate primary care mental health workers (GPCMHW) who would be trained in effective brief interventions to assist in the management and treatment of common mental health problems in all age groups. Alongside this, agreed protocols between primary and secondary care services were written to ensure that safe and effective care of people with severe mental illness was implemented. These policies were equally driven by government, users groups and the voluntary services.

Though much of the NSFMH focused on secondary or specialist mental health care, what was loud and clear was that primary care had and would continue to have a very important role to play in mental health. The workforce planning, education and training underpinning programme for adult mental health services (DH 2001) stated that: 'A number of important myths characterise past thinking about primary care mental health. These include the myths that primary care deals simply with the "worried well"; that people with severe mental illnesses are or should be managed only by specialised staff and services' (DH 2001: 98). The report also stated that the way forward was a shared value base that appreciated the bio-psychosocial model, cultural shifts to remove the barriers between services and the establishment of multidisciplinary primary care mental health teams. Many changes were taking place at the time and what was becoming evident was that mental health was coming out of the shadows to sit alongside and on par with physical illness. The introduction of the National Institute of Mental Health in England in 2001 further strengthened the mental health agenda.

Mental health service improvements began to develop and greater awareness began to prevail. Workforces such as GPs, health visitors and practice nurses who had been struggling to manage mental health issues had now begun to have their challenges recognised with specific allocated resources being granted. These included funding for primary care staff with a specific interest in mental health, training and improved liaison service. Simultaneously, the National Institute for Clinical Excellence (NICE) began to publish evidence based guidelines for the management of a number of conditions which recognised the value of psychological approaches in treatment options. Many of the guidelines also recommended that patients were treated in primary care, it being the first and to some degree the least stigmatizing option. However, as is the case with many initiatives, often demand will exceed availability. In this case, while there was some infrastructure to meet with need, it was less than sufficient as noted by the Commission for Healthcare Audit and Inspection (CHAI 2007).

The Improving Access to Psychological Therapies (IAPT) was introduced in 2006 to support the NICE guidelines for people suffering from anxiety and depression. IAPT was concerned with raising standards of recognition and treatment for people suffering from depression and anxiety disorders and aimed to give greater choice of talking therapies to those who would benefit from them (DH 2007b). Though initially IAPT focused much of its efforts on people of working age, its strategy *Talking Therapies: A Four Year Plan of Action* (DH 2011a) aims to develop and broaden its remit of providing talking therapies to all age groups. These include: those with severe mental illness, medically unexplained symptoms and those who have physical long term conditions and experience psychological distress. While the strategy incorporates principles such as improving access to services, increasing clinical recovery rates and patient choice and satisfaction, it also takes account of social factors of employment, social inclusion and participation. Other notable factors within the strategy are its commitment to equality and human rights ensuring that issues such as diversity, improving outcomes and Recovery orientated philosophies become embedded in practice and reflect both the *New Horizons* (DH 2009) and mental health outcomes strategy *No Health without Mental Health* (DH 2011b) documents.

Whereas previous government strategies have focused on an illness model of mental health, since the introduction of the NSFMH (DH 1999) there has been a gradual but steady move towards a lifespan health and wellbeing model. This model recognises the fundamental aspect of mental health as a tridirectional and integral part of human existence. While *New Horizons* (DH 2009: 7) states that its intention is 'to move towards a society where people understand that their mental well-being is as important as their physical health if they are to live their lives to the full', the mental health outcomes strategy reiterates this theme stating '*No Health without Mental Health* perfectly captures our ambitious aim to mainstream mental health in England. We are clear that we expect parity of esteem between mental and physical health services' (DH 2011b: 2). Along with the concept of wellbeing, the above statements are particularly important concepts to bear in mind when care planning and need to be incorporated into philosophies of care. Though care plans may focus on the presenting problem or need of the individual, they also need to provide strategies and interventions that will decrease the likelihood of relapse and maintain holistic wellbeing as an integral approach to living.

Activity 2.4   Critical reflection: identifying interacting systems

As a means of perpetuating proficiency, based on the example given in Figure 2.1, what other examples can you offer that demonstrate how one aspect may impact on others?

Client profile and presentations

As alluded to earlier, 90 per cent of people with mental health problems are cared for entirely in primary care. Mental illness does not present in a totally homogeneous manner and varies in intensity and severity. Epidemiological studies that examine rates often differ in their methodology and approach. It is therefore difficult to offer an exact epidemiological view of the prevalence and incidence rates of illnesses. As the scope of this chapter is beyond a detailed examination of all mental illnesses presented in primary care, this section therefore will primarily focus on depression and anxiety as they are the most common in primary care.

National guidelines would suggest that worldwide estimates of depression lie between 4 per cent and 10 per cent for major depression and between 2.5 per cent and 5 per cent for dysthymia (a chronic form of depression where moods are generally low) (NICE 2010). Though the terms 'mild' and 'moderate' depression are used in the literature and service provision frameworks (DH 2007), these terms refer to presentations that exhibit symptoms, but not to the extent that they would meet criteria for clinical criteria set in classification systems (Backenstrass et al. 2007). NICE (2009) use the following criteria in their publication *Depression in Adults with a Chronic Physical Health Problem: Treatment and Management*:

- **Subthreshold depressive symptoms**: Fewer than 5 symptoms of depression.
- **Mild depression**: Few, if any, symptoms in excess of the 5 required to make the diagnosis, and symptoms result in only minor functional impairment.
- **Moderate depression**: Symptoms or functional impairment are between 'mild' and 'severe'.
- **Severe depression**: Most symptoms, and the symptoms markedly interfere with functioning. Can occur with or without psychotic symptoms.

Note that a comprehensive assessment of depression should not rely simply on a symptom count, but should take into account the degree of functional impairment and/or disability.

(NICE 2009:11)

Anxiety is an umbrella term that encompasses a range of presentations that include: general anxiety (GAD), obsessive compulsive disorder (OCD) and phobia, panic and post traumatic stress disorders (PTSD) (APA 2000). In *Adult Psychiatric Morbidity in England: Results of a Household Survey*, McManus et al. (2009) found that more than half (9 per cent) of those with a common mental disorder presented with mixed anxiety and depressive disorder. General anxiety disorder was found in 4 per cent while 3 per cent of those surveyed screened positive for PTSD. OCD is less prevalent. Torres et al. (2006) report a 1.1 per cent prevalence rate. Skapinakis et al. (2010) assert that that prevalence rates of panic disorder with or without agoraphobiais is 1.7 per cent, with subthreshold panic being more common.

Phobias can be wide ranging and may involve animals, places, spaces or people. Social phobia (marked and persistent fear of social or performance situations) is the third most common disorder in adults worldwide with a prevalence of at least 5 per cent (Veale 2003). Considering that anxiety can be conceptualised as the overestimation of danger in context to the underestimation of coping or resources (Padesky 1997) when feeling vulnerable, it may be further elevated. In addition, as anxiety and depression often overlap or can present in a co-morbid manner, it is likely that while there may be a dominance of one, the other may also be present.

Though presentations may be deemed as mild or moderate from the patient's perspective when care planning, it is important that one considers that severity of the illness must be set in context to the patient's experience. Just as pain is considered to be as severe as the patient says it is, the same principles apply to mental illness. Though scales or inventories used to measure severity may indicate a specific level or impact and guidelines may advise certain steps or interventions, it is important to consider that severity is a personal and subjective experience. What may be disabling for one person may not be the case in the next person. People have varying coping abilities, experiences have differing meaning and people all have different views on the significance of their experiences.

As in the case of Afaf that we met earlier, depressive and anxiety disorders in the perinatal period are common. The perinatal period spans conception through to two years post partum. As Currid (2004, 2005) asserts it is a time when both mothers and partners are vulnerable to emotional changes often brought about by changing roles and dynamics in parenthood. Postnatal depression has a prevalence rate of 10–15 per cent in women with higher rates in teenage mothers (Craig and Howard 2009) and immigrant women (Collins et al. 2011). In pregnancy, rates appear to be between 5.1 (Gavin et al. 2010) and 8.4 per cent (Vesga-López et al. 2008) with increased risk in black and Asian women. Lee et al. (2007) found that anxiety was more prevalent than depression in pregnancy. Their results show that 54 per cent had anxiety compared with the 37 per cent who had depression – both being more prevalent and severe in the first and third trimester.

Though most of the research to date on perinatal distress has focused on women, men also experience distress in this period (Fletcher et al. 2006). It has been found that rates of distress amongst men in the perinatal period range from 4.8 per cent (Areias et al. 1996) in the antenatal period to 2–5 per cent in the postnatal period (Fletcher et al. 2006).

Those with long term physical health conditions also have high rates of depression. Long term conditions (LTC) are those considered to last a year or longer, that cannot be cured but can be controlled with the use of medication or other therapies (DH 2010). Conditions include coronarry heart disease, diabetes, pain related illnesses, respiratory diseases and musculoskeletal disorders. According to the Department of Health (2011b) there are around 15 million people in England with an LTC and half of those aged over 60 are diagnosed with one. Healthcare utilization for this group is high with 50 per cent of GP appointments and 70 per cent of inpatient bed days being used in the treatment and management of the varying conditions. This accounts for 70 per cent of the primary and acute care budget in England. Due to the disabling effects and prognosis of the illnesses, along with the complications, co-morbidities, suffering and constraints that people experience, it is hardly surprising that depression occurs in about 20 per cent and is two to three times more common in patients with an LTC. Egede (2007), in a study of 10,500 patients with chronic illness, found that 12 month rates of major depression were double in coronary heart failure, chronic artery disease, hypertension, and diabetes mellitus, and triple in cerebrovascular accident, chronic obstructive pulmonary disease, and end stage renal disease.

As may be expected from the prevalence rates, anxiety is also present, possibly brought about by fears of the impact of the LTC. Sareen and colleagues (2006) found that the presence of an anxiety disorder is significantly correlated with thyroid and respiratory gastrointestinal disease. Others include: arthritis, migraine headaches and allergic conditions. Other explanations for the prevalence may be both the bi-directional pathology and course of the disease.

Having physical health issues may further predispose or precipitate mental illness. This can be due to a number of bi- or tri-directional interactions. For example, someone who is in constant pain may feel helpless and consider that there is no hope of the pain ever subsiding and as a result find socializing difficult. Other examples where these directional interactions are evident include symptoms of depression in hypothyroidism, anaemia and hyperglycemia; anxiety symptoms in hyperthyroidism; and panic in chronic obstructive pulmonary disease. Therefore as mentioned earlier in the holism in practice section, to prevent overshadowing it is imperative that one remains focused on the individual's experience rather than their diagnosis. However knowledge of co-morbidities will be useful in assessment of the individual as it may be part of a behavioural phenotype – a heightened probability that people with a given syndrome will exhibit behavioural or developmental sequelae relative to others without the syndrome, for example, depression in Fragile X and Coffin Lowry syndrome (McNamara 2011) in people with a learning disability.

Cooper et al. (2007) found the point prevalence (a measure of the proportion of people who have a condition at a particular time) of mental ill health in a sample of 1032 people with intellectual difficulties to be 40.9 per cent. While the NHS evidence website recognises that depression does occur in people with learning disabilities, it highlights that studies to detect prevalence show marked variance possibly due to the question as to whether the diagnostic criteria used for those without a learning disability are appropriate for those with a learning disability. Despite this, Prasher (1999) asserts that the rate of depression could possibly be twice that of the general population and certainly not less common. Setting in context to possible vulnerabilities and experiences of people with a learning disability, a range of factors may add to an increased likelihood. These include: social factors – isolation, stigma or exclusion and psychological factors – cognitive and communication difficulties that may impair their ability to understand experiences or relay their feelings. Biological factors – organic causes of the presentation – may further predispose the individual to other mental illnesses, for example, those with Down's syndrome develop brain changes associated with Alzheimer's disease (Alvarez 2011).

Depression and dementia may have similar symptoms. These include memory loss, difficulties in concentration, loss of interest and other cognitive impairment. There is also evidence of a correlation of dementia following depression and evidence suggests that having depression may double the risk of developing dementia. In a prospective designed study conducted over 17 years, the Framingham Heart Study (Saczynski et al. 2010) found that 21.6 per cent of participants who were depressed at baseline developed dementia compared with 16.6 per cent of non-depressed participants and that depressed participants had more than a 50 per cent increased risk. Though there is a lack of consensus as to how best to define anxiety in dementia due to symptom overlap, anxiety is also prevalent in dementia with estimated rates ranging from 5 to 21 per cent for disorders and 8 to 71 per cent for anxiety symptoms (Seignourel et al. 2008). Neville and Teri (2011) support the above and also suggest that a lack of competence and negative staff reactions to patients' behaviours may contribute to increasing anxiety severity.

Two other areas where both anxiety and depression are prevalent are in medically unexplained symptoms (MUS) and palliative care. Palliative care is a period where clinicians involved strive to improve the life of patients suffering with life threatening illness by intervening early to relieve suffering. As may be understood, many people in this category suffer greatly both in terms of physical and psychological pain as well as social adversities at the time of diagnosis and the course of the illness. The NICE guidelines further elaborate stating:

> Around the time of a diagnosis of cancer, approximately half of all patients experience levels of anxiety and depression severe enough to affect their quality of life adversely. About one quarter continue to be so affected during the following six months. Among those who experience recurrence of disease, the prevalence of anxiety and depression rises to 50 per cent and remains at this level throughout the course of advanced illness. In the year following diagnosis, around one in ten patients will experience symptoms severe enough to warrant intervention by specialist psychological/psychiatric services. Such symptoms can also be seen in 10–15 per cent of patients with advanced disease.
>
> (NICE 2004: 74)

A range of feelings may be evident from anger and guilt to worry. Verbal responses may sometimes indicate these feelings: 'why me?','if only I hadn't', 'what if?'. However, despite what may be an obvious distressing and emotionally difficult time for patients, depression often goes unrecognised (Lloyd-Williams and Riddleston 2002; Rayner et al. 2009).

MUS are described as physical symptoms that have no known physical pathological cause (IAPT 2008). They are common across general medicine and are about twice as likely to fulfil criteria for mental disorders (Nimnuan et al. 2001). Up to

70 per cent of people with MUS will suffer from anxiety or depression (IAPT 2008). MUS increase healthcare utilization with studies showing that between 20 and 30 per cent of people who are experiencing MUS present in primary care. This figure increases to an average of 52 per cent in secondary care where many investigations and further consultations take place (IAPT 2011). MUS is a difficult clinical, conceptual and emotional area for practitioners as they may feel their competence is challenged to explain the symptoms (Hatcher and Arroll 2008). As a consequence, patients presenting with these symptoms have been described in derogatory terms or may not be offered the treatments required. Having the ability to comprehensively assess and conceptualise cases is key to care planning activity; without it your treatments may not be effective.

Care planning

For this section on care planning, we will use the following case study of Jean to illustrate the application of theory to practice. There are a number of assessment strategies that can be undertaken to gain a global overview of the difficulties that Jean may be experiencing. Lloyd (2010) offers many practical approaches to gain both a holistic and a specific assessment of patients' difficulties that are applicable in a number of care settings or services. This section will primarily focus on planning care set in the context of the template below.

Case study – Jean

Jean is a 50-year-old who got divorced six months ago. She has two daughters aged 22 and 19. The eldest daughter lives with her father, and the youngest lives in the university's halls of residence where she has recently started. Jean has been depressed over the last six months and has been experiencing panic attacks for over eight months. She has started her menopause and it has been observed that her thyroxine levels are low. Jean is finding it increasingly difficult to go out and has not worked for over six weeks. She is very embarrassed by the fact that she is divorced and gets anxious at the thought of telling her parents. Though they live close by and her father is the local vicar, she rarely sees them.

She sees her ex-husband almost daily and he is now doing most of her shopping and running other errands. Her daughters spend the weekend with her and phone her every evening. She has stopped socializing, believing that her work colleagues are just being sympathetic and really would not want her 'moping around them'. In addition, she is fearful that she will have a panic attack and her friends may think she is 'crazy'.

Conceptualizing

Conceptualizing the issues or problems presented is the cornerstone of planning care and treatment. In this sense, conceptualizing may be defined as the process of gathering information in a manner that provides greater depth of understanding of the issue at hand and takes account of other factors or dynamics, which in turn will offer a more accurate representation of the problem. This will involve actively listening and asking questions that will provide you with a fuller account of the mechanisms of distress. To do so, it is important to consider the following. Patients' subjective personal accounts may not always be the only account and levels of distress may influence how we perceive the world. Therefore, if it is permissible by the patient, it may be useful to ask a significant other for input as it will add to the objectivity. It is also worth noting that we may be so preoccupied with managing the distress that we have not stopped to think about the mechanisms or how it manifests. Secondly, as professionals we may be influenced by theoretical assumptions or previous cases which, though helpful, may prevent us from approaching our patient in a unique manner. For example, in Jean's case we may immediately think that her distress is caused by her divorce, menopause and hypothyroidism. While these may be contributing factors, we need to bear in mind other possibilities. Often, it may be that the presenting problem is not the problem per se, but rather the consequence of the problem, as will be seen later. In addition, it is also important to ask yourself questions such as 'Why is this happening now?', 'When, where or how does it come about?', 'What may be the issues keeping this going?' The following Ps framework (Table 2.1) may help in gaining a more detailed understanding of Jean. This framework is drawn from several professions including health psychology (Nikcevic et al. 2006), cognitive behaviour therapy (Persons 2008) and nursing (Callaghan and Waldock 2006; Newell and Gournay 2009). Jean's case is used to illustrate its application.

To gain a further understanding of the operational aspect of this, the following As framework based on the work of Padesky and Mooney (1990) and Garland et al. (2002) is offered. The operational aspect is drawn from Clark's (1986) cognitive model of panic attacks and Elliot's (1999) Approach-Avoidance motivation theory.

- **Antecedents** Past: criticism from parents; recent: sitting at home thinking about how she will tell her parents that she is divorced;
- **Appraisal** Thinks that they will further criticise her and be unsupportive and malevolent;
- **Affective** Feels anxious and jittery;
- **Approach (to solve bad feelings)** Continues to think of 'best way' to tell them; which will bring the least amount of criticism;
- **Autonomic/auto receptor** Palpitations, perspiration, difficulty in breathing – resulting in a panic attack;
- **After-effect** The distress of her panic attack makes her feel vulnerable and she begins to believe that she could not cope if this happens away

Table 2.1 The Ps framework

Predisposing factors	What are the past experiences or issues that may be influencing this?	Past experiences of being criticised by her mother and told that she'd (Jean) never make a good wife.
Precipitating factors	What are the more recent issues that may have triggered this? Ask yourself 'Why now?'	Not yet having told her parents of her divorce and fearing the situation of when she tells them.
Perpetuating factors	What are the issues that keep this problem going?	Not yet having told them and then sitting for long periods thinking about the possible consequences of telling them and how best to tell them.
Protective factors	What are the issues that stop deterioration or help in this problem e.g. social supports, relationships?	Ex-husband and daughters are caring and Jean has strong relationships with them.
Problem development	How has this problem developed, what were the early experiences or onset?	Past criticism by parents for not being as good as her siblings. Later criticisms about her ability to be a good wife and ongoing criticisms about her abilities in general and how these have negative reflections on Jean's parents and siblings.
Presenting problem	At first glance what is the problem or the consequences of above factors?	Panic attacks, not being able to go out, depression.
Problem identification	What has been identified collaboratively that is more accurate of the real issue?	When Jean thinks about meeting her parents and telling them that she is now divorced, she experiences panic attacks which frighten her and make her think she is 'going crazy'. As a means of avoiding her parents and dealing with the panic attacks, she has stopped going out.

from home. She avoids going out which gives her temporary relief, but the long term consequence is that the more she avoids going out, the more difficult it is to go out.

As illustrated, past and recent antecedents give rise to appraisals that are the precursor to anxious feelings. Jean's problem-solving approach to dealing with these distressing experiences is to continue to think of the 'best way' to tell her parents about her divorce. However, as you can see, the more Jean thinks, the more anxious she becomes which ultimately ends in a panic attack. As a result of the severe distress she feels more vulnerable and starts to think about what she'd do if this happened outside. She believes she wouldn't cope so her solution is to stay indoors. However, while her avoidance provides a solution to ensuring a panic attack does not happen outside, it also brings about the consequences of staying indoors and never having a chance to test whether she would cope with a panic attack or whether it may even occur.

Based on the additional information, in the new care plan, the collaborative agreed need is altered to reflect a more accurate representation that takes account of a number of other aspects. However, as mentioned earlier, this will only be arrived at if you work closely with your patient for you both to discover the finer detail and make sense of the presenting issue. As indicated, Jean is beginning to discover that it is fear that is preventing her from going out and that is the mechanism that contributes to its maintenance.

Setting goals

Distress can be overwhelming and people use a variety of approaches to help them cope. While some may be adaptable in nature, others may not. The intention of these strategies is to reduce or alleviate the agonizing feelings that arise from the distress. Though maladaptive strategies prove useful in the short term, the longer term consequences can be even more disabling and counterproductive. As we saw in Afaf's case, drinking alcohol helped her initially; however in the long term she may become dependent on it to deal with crises. It is imperative to understand that these strategies have become the person's coping mechanisms and any interference or attempt to change them may be uncomfortable and anxiety provoking. It is not unusual to meet with resistance. Remember, as problems take time to develop, learning alternative helpful strategies also takes time to master. Therefore goals need to be set in a sensitive patient directed manner and paced in achievable and realistic steps. Other factors that need to be considered are the gradient of difficulty and the level of discomfort that the patient may feel due to the changes occurring. Sensitivity is the key here. You may find that as goals are achieved, the patient may want to increase the pace or the gradient of difficulty that is required to meet with their ultimate goal.

In Jean's case, the longer term goal is for her to be able to go out alone. In order to master this, a number of smaller systematic steps need to be repeatedly undertaken. The goals have been written in a SMARTT (specific, measurable, achievable realistic, timely and tangible) form, however, it must be remembered that we cannot see into the future and it may be necessary to review the goals depending on Jean's ability. Finally, goals for other issues do need to complement one another and contribute to the ultimate goal of restoring Jean's health. In this case, as Jean is also presenting with depressive like symptoms, her goals would include going out mixing with friends to increase pleasure and also challenge her thinking that they didn't want her 'moping around' them.

Evidence based interventions and their rationale

The National Institute for Health and Clinical Exellence (NICE) provide a number of guidelines for a variety of presentations and conditions in their quest to promote good health and prevent illness. These guidelines are based on the best available evidence and assist practitioners to have the confidence and meet with standards set by their regulatory bodies. It is now common practice and an expectation that practitioners follow these guidelines. However, while there are many advantages and merits of using evidence based practice, in some situations, studies that have sought to provide evidence are not yet in a position to draw a conclusion and the evidence may not yet be available. Also, it must be noted that some studies seek to generalise their findings and there are occasions where findings may not apply to your particular client. If for example you wanted to use the best available evidence to greet someone, you may find that the literature advises shaking hands, maintaining eye contact and smiling. However, culturally this may not be suitable, for some patients. In the absence of evidence based guidelines, we must seek to ensure that what we are doing has a sound rationale that is acceptable, logical and justifiable to our patient. In addition, the interventions need to be devised in partnership with the patient and practitioners need to be cognisant that while they have expertise, patients also have expertise. Otherwise, we may find that patients will not engage or they become passive recipients in their care thus disadvantaging them of the opportunity to learn and master problem solving techniques. Table 2.2 provides an example of how such collaborative care planning can be devised.

In the hypothetical case of Jean, the interventions offered have been informed by a number of sources. These include Government guidelines, chapters from books, journal articles and reflective practice. In real life situations, Jean would also input heavily into the interventions and together we would share our expertise in overcoming her difficulties. This reciprocal arrangement has benefits for both parties. From a patient's perspective, they will learn new strategies that can be used in future life situations, while for the practitioner, they can further learn about presentations, difficulties that may be experienced and also alternative or new ways of working to overcome difficulties encountered.

Health promotion and further resources

Helping patients with issues should not be seen as isolated incidents but rather as the contribution from the dependence to independence continuum. Ultimately, the philosophy is to empower the patient to become their own wellbeing practitioner. As mentioned earlier, we are seeing a move away from the paternalistic models of illness to one that focuses on adopting responsibility and choice for wellbeing. Commensurate with this, we need to focus on providing the preventative and proactive resources to do this. By exploring and providing information on relapse signatures and self-help material, patients are given the opportunity to identify earlier the signs that they may be relapsing or developing difficulties. In

Table 2.2 Care plan for Jean

Assessment	Planning	Implementation	Evaluation
Jean's fear of having a panic attack and not coping results in her staying indoors. This avoidance of going out prevents her from testing her belief about coping with a panic attack outside	*Short Term Goal* Jean will learn and master panic management strategies that she can use to overcome the distress felt	1 Develop and sustain a relationship with Jean based on recovery values and self-help principles 2 Ask Jean to keep a diary of her panic attacks noting the onset, antecedents, severity and duration	6 weeks by care coordinator
	Intermediate Goal Over the next twelve weeks Jean will initially go out with the practitioner for short periods of time which will gradually be lengthened at Jean's pace	3 Embark on a psycho-educational programme that will assist both Jean and the practitioner to make sense of the issue while collaboratively working together to discover and conceptualise the presenting issues	12 weeks by care coordinator
	Later in the outings, panic-like symptoms will be evoked to enable Jean to use and master her new learnt panic management strategies	4 Teach Jean controlled breathing exercises, progressive muscle relaxation, shifting her focus of attention away from the panic attack and increasing her pleasurable activities to distract and lessen time thinking about her parents' possible reactions	
	Long Term Goal Jean will go outdoors alone and will have mastered a number of coping strategies to manage panic attacks if they occur, in four months' time	5 Use strategies that will challenge Jean's thoughts such as thought records and asking for evidence that her thoughts are accurate 6 Explore alternatives ways of dealing with criticisms 7 Build a programme with Jean that gradually reintroduces going outdoors, lengthening the duration each time and ensuring that she stays in the environment despite her feeling anxious 8 Plan opportunities for Jean to practise her panic management strategies 9 Plan successive unaccompanied outings and review successes and difficulties 10 Build strategies to manage difficulties.	

doing so, early intervention will have untold benefits, the least of which is reducing the levels of distress and adversities to their quality of life. Fortunately there are many websites, computer based programs, self-help books and groups that are available to support those experiencing distress. The added advantage of this approach is that a patient can gain instant access, take control of their treatment and choose which approach to take or which will best suit them. Further, it is a less stigmatizing option for those who may not want mental health services.

Using signatures in a care plan is a method of ensuring agreement between those involved in the care and provides consent from the patient. It also demonstrates a commitment by all to effect seamless quality care that will bring meaningful and lasting change and will improve the future quality of the individual's life and hope.

Activity 2.5   Critical reflection: putting it altogether

Using Jean's case, try to complete a care plan that will address her low mood. Remember to include the APIE framework to help you organise the care plan and demonstrate SMART care planning.

Conclusion

Primary care mental health is the largest area of mental health provision. Presentations are varied and can be challenging, particularly for those who may not have the expertise to deliver the care required. More recently, specific initiatives to address these variations and challenges have been introduced in government policy. Underpinning these policies are commitments of acknowledging that mental health is as important as physical health, moving from an illness model of mental health to a wellbeing model, and increasing access to mental health services. To effect this, the workforce needs to embrace contemporary mental health practice, which may involve moving away from traditional methods to evidence based approaches. These include working alongside patients as equal partners and providing information which will make sense of the patients' distress. This will then enable patients to make meaningful informed choices about their treatments, empower them and further their expertise in managing their own distress. Recovery principled care planning provides a golden opportunity as a vehicle to deliver this vision along with meeting many more agendas of mental health care.

References

Academy of Medical Royal Colleges (2009) *No Health Without Mental Health*. London: Royal College of Psychiatrists.

Alvarez, N. (2011) *Alzheimer's Disease in Individuals with Down Syndrome*. http://www.emedicinehealth.com/alzheimer_disease_in_individuals_with_down_syndro/article_em.htm (accessed 6 February 2012).

American Psychiatric Association (2000) *Diagnostic and Statistical Manual of Mental Disorders*, 4th edn, text revision. Washington, DC: American Psychiatric Association.

Areias, M.E.G., Kumar, R., Barros, H. and Figueiredo, E. (1996) Correlates of postnatal depression in mothers and fathers. *British Journal of Psychiatry*, 169: 36–41.

Armstrong, E. (2001) The primary/secondary care interface, in C. Brooker and J. Repper (eds) *Serious Mental Health Problems in the Community: Policy, Practice and Research*. London: Baillière Tindall.

Backenstrass, M., Joest, K., Rosemann, T. and Szecsenyi, J. (2007) The care of patients with subthreshold depression in primary care: is it all that bad? A qualitative study on the views of general practitioners and patients. *BMC Health Service Research*, 7: 190.

Barker, P. (2003) The tidal model: psychiatric colonization, recovery and the paradigm shift in mental health care. *International Journal of Mental Health Nursing*, 12: 96–102.

Borrell-Carrió, F., Suchman, A.L. and Epstein, R.M. (2004) The biopsychosocial model 25 years later: principles, practice, and scientific inquiry. *Annals of Family Medicine*, 2: 576–82.

Burns, T. and Priebe, S. (1999) Mental health care failure in England. *British Journal of Psychiatry*, 174: 191–2.

Byrne, P. (2000) Stigma of mental illness and ways of diminishing it. *Advances in Psychiatric Treatment*, 6: 65–72.

Callaghan, P. and Waldock, H. (eds) (2006) *Oxford Handbook of Mental Health Nursing*. Oxford: Oxford University Press.

Care Quality Commission (2011) *The State of Health Care and Adult Social Care in England: An Overview of Key Themes in Care 2009/10*. London: TSO.

Clark, D.M. (1986) A cognitive approach to panic. *Behaviour Research and Therapy*, 24: 461–70.

Collins, C., Zimmerman, C. and Howard, L.M. (2011) Refugee, asylum seeker, immigrant women and postnatal depression: rates and risk factors. *Archives of Women's Mental Health*, 14: 3–11.

Commission for Healthcare Audit and Inspection (2007) *No Voice, No Choice: A Joint Review of Adult Community Mental Health Services in England*. London: Healthcare Commission and Commission for Social Care Inspection.

Cooper, S.A., Smiley, E. and Morrison, J. et al. (2007) Mental ill-health in adults with intellectual disabilities: prevalence and associated factors. *British Journal of Psychiatry*, 190: 27–35.

Craig, M.C. and Howard, L. (2009) Postnatal depression, *British Medical Journal – Clinical Evidence*. http://ukpmc.ac.uk/articles/PMC2 07780 (accessed 5 February 2012).

Currid, T. (2003) The role of mental health education in a primary care setting, *Nursing Times*, 99(9): 48–9.

Currid, T. (2004) Improving perinatal mental health care. *Nursing Standard*, 19(3): 40–3.

Currid, T.J. (2005) Psychological issues surrounding paternal perinatal mental health. *Nursing Times*, 101: 40–2.

Curtice, M., Symonds, R. and Exworthy, T. (2010) *FREDA – A Human Rights-based Approach to Clinical Practice*. http://www.psychiatrycpd.co.uk/pdf/FREDA%20 human%20rights-based%20approach%20to%20clinical%20practice_THN.pdf (accessed 6 February 2012).

DH (Department of Health) (1995) *Building Bridges: A Guide to Arrangements For Inter-agency Working for the Care and Protection of Severely Mentally Ill People*. London: Department of Health.

DH (1999) *National Service Framework for Mental Health: Modern Standards and Service Models*. http://www.dh.gov.uk/prod_consum_dh/groups/dh_digitalassets/ @dh/@en/documents/digitalasset/dh_4077209.pdf (accessed 6 February 2012).

DH (2000) *The NHS Plan: A Plan for Investment, a Plan for Reform*. http://www.dh. gov.uk/prod_consum_dh/groups/dh_digitalassets/@dh/@en/@ps/documents/ digitalasset/dh_118522.pdf (accessed 6 February 2012).

DH (2001) *Mental Health National Service Framework (and the NHS Plan) Workforce Planning, Education and Training Underpinning Programme: Adult Mental Health Services: Final Report by the Workforce Action Team*. http://www.dh.gov.uk/ prod_consum_dh/groups/dh_digitalassets/@dh/@en/documents/digitalasset/ dh_4085653.pdf (accessed 6 February 2012).

DH (2007a) *Commissioning a Brighter Future: Improving Access to Psychological Therapies*. Care Services Improvement Partnership, National Institute for Mental Health England. http://www.iapt.nhs.uk/silo/files/commissioning-a-brighter-future.pdf (accessed 6 February 2012).

DII (2007b) *Improving Access to Psychological Therapies: Specifications for the Commissioner-led Pathfinder Programme*. http://www.iapt.nhs.uk/silo/files/ specification-for-the-commissionerled-pathfinder-programme.pdf (accessed 6 February 2012).

DH (2009) *New Horizons: A Shared Vision for Mental Health*. http://www.dh.gov.uk/ prod_consum_dh/groups/dh_digitalassets/@dh/@en/documents/digitalasset/ dh_109708.pdf (accessed 6 February 2012).

DH (2010) *Improving the Health and Well-being of People with Long Term Conditions*. London: TSO.

DH (2011a) *Talking Therapies: A Four-year Plan of Action. A Supporting Document to No Health Without Mental Health: A Cross-Government Mental Health Outcomes Strategy for People of all Ages*. http://www.dh.gov.uk/prod_consum_dh/groups/ dh_digitalassets/documents/digitalasset/dh_123985.pdf (accessed 6 February 2012)

DH (2011b) *No Health Without Mental Health: A Cross-Government Mental Health Outcomes Strategy for People of all Ages*. http://www.dh.gov.uk/ prod_consum_dh/groups/dh_digitalassets/documents/digitalasset/dh_124058 .pdf (accessed 6 February 2012).

Egede, L.E. (2007) Major depression in individuals with chronic medical disorders: prevalence, and correlates and associates of health resource utilisation, lost productivity and functional disability. *General Hospital Psychiatry*, 29: 409–16.

Elliot, A.J. (1999) Approach and avoidance motivation and achievement goals. *Educational Psychologist*, 34: 169–89.

Engel, G.L. (1977) The need for a new medical model: a challenge for biomedicine. *Science (New Series)*, 196: 129–36.

Fletcher, R.J., Matthey, S. and Marley, C.G., (2006) Addressing depression and anxiety among new fathers. *Medical Journal of Australia*, 185: 461–3.

Garland, A., Fox, R. and Williams, C.J. (2002) Overcoming reduced activity and avoidance: a five areas approach. *Advances in Psychiatric Treatment*, 8(6): 453–62.

Gavin, A.R., Melville, J.L., Rue, T. et al. (2010) Racial differences in the prevalence of antenatal depression. *General Hospital Psychiatry*, 3(6): 87–93. http://www.cfah.org/hbns/archives/viewSupportDoc.cfm?supportingDocID=1006 (accessed 6 February 2012).

Goffman, E. (1963) *Stigma: Notes on the Management of Spoiled Identity*. Englewood Cliffs, NJ: Prentice-Hall.

Halter, M.J. (2008) Perceived characteristics of psychiatric nurses: stigma by association. *Archives of Psychiatric Nursing*, 22: 20–6.

Hatcher, S. and Arroll, B. (2008) Assessment and management of medically unexplained symptoms. *British Medical Journal*, 336: 1124–8. http://www.dh.gov.uk/prod_consum_dh/groups/dh_digitalassets/@dh/@en/@ps/documents/digitalasset/dh_111187.pdf (accessed 6 February 2012).

Improving Access to Psychological Therapies (2008) *Positive Practice Guide*. http://www.iapt.nhs.uk/silo/files/medically-unexplained-symptoms-positive-practice-guide.pdf (accessed 6 February 2012).

Improving Access to Psychological Therapies (2011) *Medically Unexplained Symptoms*. http://www.iapt.nhs.uk/special-interests/medically-unexplained-symptoms (accessed 6 February 2012).

King's Fund (2011) *Mental Health: Key Issues*. http://www.kingsfund.org.uk/topics/mental_health/#keypoints (accessed 6 February 2012).

Lee, A.M., Lam, S.K., Sze Mun Lau, S. et al. (2007). Prevalence, course and risk factors for antenatal anxiety and depression. *Obstetrics and Gynecology*, 110: 1102–12.

Lloyd, M. (2010) *A Practical Guide to Care Planning in Health and Social Care*. Maidenhead: Open University Press.

Lloyd-Williams, M. and Riddleston, H. (2002) The stability of depression scores in patients who are receiving palliative care. *Journal of Pain Symptom Management*, 24(6): 593–7.

McNamara, E. (2011) *Mental and Behavioural Disorders in Adults with a Learning Disability*. Hertfordshire MRCPsych Course. http://www.docstoc.com/docs/20951864/MENTAL-DISORDERS-IN-MENTAL-RETARDATION (accessed 6 February 2012).

McCormick, A., Fleming, D. and Charlton, J. (1995) *Morbidity Statistics from General Practice: Fourth National Study 1991–1992*. London: HMSO, series MB5 no. 3.

McManus, S., Meltzer, H., Brugha, T., Bebbington, P. and Jenkins, R. (2009) *Adult Psychiatric Morbidity in England, 2007: Results of a Household Survey*. Leads: NHS Information Centre for Health and Social Care.

Michael, J. (2008) *Healthcare for All, Report of the Independent Inquiry into Access to Healthcare for People with Learning Disabilities*. http://www.dh.gov.uk/prod_consum_dh/groups/dh_digitalassets/@dh/@en/documents/digitalasset/dh_106126.pdf

National Institute for Health and Clinical Excellence (2004) *Guidance on Cancer Services: Improving Supportive and Palliative Care for Adults with Cancer: The Manual*. http://www.nice.org.uk/nicemedia/pdf/csgspmanual.pdf

National Institute for Health and Clinical Excellence (2009) *Depression in Adults with a Chronic Physical Health Problem: Treatment and Management*. http://www.nice.org.uk/nicemedia/pdf/CG91NICEGuideline.pdf

National Institute for Health and Clinical Excellence (2010) *Depression: The NICE Guidelines on the Treatment and Management of Depression in Adults*, updated edition. http://www.nice.org.uk/nicemedia/live/12329/45896/45896.pdf

Neville, C. and Teri, L. (2011) Anxiety, anxiety symptoms, and associations among older people with dementia in assisted-living facilities. *International Journal of Mental Health Nursing*, 20(3): 195–201.

Newell, R. and Gournay, K. (eds) (2009) *Mental Health Nursing: An Evidence Based Approach*. Edinburgh: Churchill Livingstone. http://www.evidence.nhs.uk/nhs-evidence-content/important-new-evidence/learning-disabilities (accessed 6 February 2012).

Nikcevic, A.V., Kuczmierczyk, A.R. and Bruch, M. (eds) (2006) *Formualtion and Treatment in Clinical Psychology*. New York: Routledge.

Nimnuan, C., Hotopf, M. and Wessely, S. (2001) Medically unexplained symptoms: an epidemiological study in seven specialities. *Journal of Psychosomatic Research*, 51: 361–7.

Office of the Children's Commissioner (2007) *Pushed into the Shadows: Young People's Experience of Adult Mental Health Facilities*. The Children's Commissioner for England. http://www.teespublichealth.nhs.uk/Download/Public/1012/DOCUMENT/4721/Pushed%20into%20the%20Shadows.pdf (accessed 6 February 2012).

Onyett, S.R. (2003) *Teamworking in Mental Health*. Basingstoke: Palgrave Macmillan.

Padesky, C. (1997) A more effective treatment focus for social phobia? *International Cognitive Therapy Newsletter*, 11(1): 1–3. http://www.padesky.com/clinicalcorner/pdf/social_phobia.PDF (accessed 6 February 2012).

Padesky, C.A. and Mooney, K.A. (1990) Clinical tip: presenting the cognitive model to clients. *International Cognitive Therapy Newsletter*, 6: 13–14.

Persons, J. (2008) *The Case Formulation Approach to Cognitive Behaviour Therapy*. New York: Guilford Press.

Prasher, V. (1999) Presentation and management of depression in people with learning disability. *Advances in Psychiatric Treatment*, 5: 447–54.

Rayner, L., Loge, J.H., Wasteson, E. and Higgson, I. (2009) The detection of depression in palliative care. *Current Opinion in Supportive and Palliative Care*, 3(1): 55–60.

Royal College of Psychiatrists (2008) *Fair Deal for Mental Health: Our Manifesto for a 3 Year Campaign Dedicated to Tackling Inequality in Mental Healthcare.* http://www.rcpsych.ac.uk/pdf/Fair%20Deal%20manifesto%20(full%20-%201st%20July2009).pdf.pdf (accessed 6 February 2012).

Saczynski, J.S., Beiser, A., Seshadri, S. et al. (2010) Depressive symptoms and risk of dementia: the Framingham Heart Study. *Neurology*, 75: 35–41.

Sareen, J., Jacobi, F., Cox, B.J. et al. (2006) Disability and poor quality of life associated with comorbid anxiety disorders and physical conditions. *Archives of Internal Medicine*, 166: 2109–16.

Seignourel, P., Kunik, M., Snow, L., Wilson, N. and Stanley, M. (2008) Anxiety in dementia: a critical review. *Clinical Psychology Review*, 28: 1071–82.

Skapinakis, P., Lewis, G., Davies, S. et al. (2010) Panic disorder and subthreshold panic in the UK general population: epidemiology, comorbidity and functional limitation. *European Psychiatry*, 26(6): 354–62.

Torres, A.R., Prince, M.J., Bebbington, P. et al. (2006) Obsessive–compulsive disorder: prevalence, comorbidity, impact, and help-seeking in the British National Psychiatric Morbidity Survey of 2000. *American Journal of Psychiatry*, 163(11): 1978–85.

Veale, D. (2003) Treatment of social phobia. *Advances in Psychiatric Treatment*, 9: 258–64.

Vesga-López, O., Blanco, C., Keyes, K. et al. (2008) Psychiatric disorders in pregnant and postpartum women in the United States. *Archives of General Psychiatry*, 65(7): 805–15.

3 Care planning in the community

Neil Robdale

Learning outcomes

After reading this chapter you will be able to

- Discuss the Care Programme Approach and how it is implemented in mental health practice
- Describe the need for interagency and multidisciplinary team working
- Identify how policy and law influences mental health care
- Discuss assessment and care planning in the community setting

Introduction

Care planning in community mental health is a very wide arena. Increasingly since the 1980s mental health services have been moving away from hospital based to community based treatment (Cronin-Davis and Long 2006). In the early 1990s community mental health teams were set up, which tended to be all embracing in terms of taking all mental health referrals from GPs and from hospital services. By the beginning of the twenty-first century the process of decreasing hospital beds and increasing community care had gathered pace. Alongside this there came the development of different specialist mental health teams. Since the early 2000s specialist teams have been developed for early intervention in psychosis, home treatment and crisis intervention teams, primary care liaison and assertive outreach teams. There are numerous other community teams in mental health specializing in eating disorders, dual diagnosis, substance misuse or rehabilitation and recovery. Working in the community could mean working in any one of these areas but what they all share is a need to follow a care pathway and to create an appropriate care plan.

In this chapter I will explain the main issues in creating a care plan. It will be mainly from the perspective of working in a community mental health team. This will give a broad idea of creating a care plan in the community but it would need to be adapted in applying it to other specialist teams. Before looking directly at creating a care plan, we will explore the many issues that are particularly relevant to this process in community mental health.

Throughout this chapter I will use a case study to highlight various points. This case study will be based on a variety of real experiences and incidents.

Case study – Graham

Graham is a 29-year-old man who lives alone in a one bedroomed flat in a large town. He dropped out from university at the age of 20. He had become very stressed and had indulged heavily in alcohol and cannabis. He developed paranoid ideas and delusions and was given a diagnosis of schizophrenia. He takes oral medication on a daily basis.

Initially he returned to live with his parents but he is now living in his own flat. He sees his parents occasionally. He still uses alcohol and illegal drugs on a fairly regular basis. He is a heavy smoker.

He has tried a few temporary jobs over the intervening years but is now unemployed. He has difficulty getting up in the morning, keeping to time schedules and motivating himself. In general his level of activity is low. He tends to isolate himself and has few friends.

His hygiene and self-care are poor. His flat is generally cluttered and grimy. He is generally keen on recycling but this leads him to hoard everything rather than throw anything away. He has even gone to the extent of collecting other people's rubbish and storing it in his flat.

Most of his money goes on cigarettes and alcohol, which leads him to get into debt.

The Care Programme Approach

Graham would come under the auspices of the Care Programme Approach (CPA). This was first introduced in 1991 to help provide the basis for the care of people with mental health needs (Care Programme Approach Association 2008). To enable this to happen the health trusts and local authority social services have to work together to supply a care package which targets the needs of the individual service user and their carers. The care coordinator will be the person responsible for implementing the Care Programme Approach and for producing the care plan and having regular reviews of this. The CPA brought about the creation of the care coordinator, whose responsibility it is to ensure that the service user receives the services that they are entitled to (DH 2006).

The CPA put in place a system of working to ensure minimum standards of assessment and review for users of mental health services. It entitles everyone referred to mental health services to an assessment of their needs and for those with ongoing issues or enduring mental health needs a system of regular review.

This review period is set at a minimum of every 12 months but local policies may dictate other time-frames such as six monthly.

Another element of the CPA system is to ensure that service users, who may move from one part of the country to another, receive the care they are entitled to and they do not fall through the mental health net. There is a responsibility for the care coordinator to inform the mental health services in the area to which the service user has moved. Clearly there is an element of monitoring, as well as support, built into this system.

The issues of care coordination and good communication become integral to each other in ensuring the process of review. The system of CPA review is the main tool for recording the progress of the service user and for updating the care plan. For a review of a person's care plan the care coordinator should set up a date for the review and invite all relevant parties to the review. The list of those involved could clearly be very expansive including:

- service user
- care coordinator
- psychiatrist
- general practitioner
- support services
- housing services
- carers
- service user advocate.

The practicality of getting so many people together in one place at one time can prove to be extremely difficult. Often only the three or four key people will attend and information will be gathered from those not attending. The summary of the review can be sent out to all relevant parties in order to keep everyone abreast of the current position with indicators for future action.

Care coordination

Graham would have a care coordinator at the team responsible for his care. The role of the care coordinator is key in the community setting. It is exactly as it sounds. The role is to coordinate the care for an individual service user. The role is a generic one and could be carried out by a nurse, social worker, occupational therapist or psychologist. It involves clear communication within the immediate team and colleagues, but also with all other agencies involved with the individual's care. When thinking of care you need to think holistically, as this covers all aspects of a service user's life. The definition will incorporate all health and social care. It will cover medical treatments and interventions, mental health support, housing, domestic support, welfare benefits, dealing with gas, electric and water companies and anything else that appears to interfere with the individual's good mental health.

In terms of health care the main agency the coordinator will be liaising with will be the multidisciplinary team (MDT) which will usually consist of:

- consultant psychiatrist and other grade psychiatrist;
- community mental health nurses;
- occupational therapists;
- social workers;
- psychologist;
- care workers or STaR workers (support time and recovery).

Enabling a service user to access the benefits that they are entitled to will be one of the care coordinator's responsibilities. This would certainly be an important element for Graham, who has difficulty managing his money and dealing with the appropriate council or government agencies. This will involve helping to order and fill in application forms and telephone calls to chase things up and for clarification. As we all know making telephone calls to call centres can be a very frustrating process, with numerous numerical options, being kept waiting listening to random pieces of music and eventually getting cut off. If we can get frustrated by this, imagine having a mental health problem on top of this. Imagine having a lack of motivation or energy. Imagine having extreme anxiety about talking to other people and avoiding any outside contact. These are the service users you will be supporting to deal with these bureaucratic agencies.

There may be specialised services within the local council who also help people deal with benefits issues and you will need to liaise with these. These range from Citizens Advice Bureau (CAB) to local government welfare benefit departments or specific disability support agencies. They may be able to visit the service user at home and help them complete important application forms and offer specialised advice on entitlements to benefits. The CAB usually provides a specialist section which helps people with debts.

Activity 3.1   Critical reflection

The question is often asked whether you as a mental health professional should help someone like Graham access benefits, when you are fairly sure that he will spend the extra money on drugs, alcohol or cigarettes.
    What do you think?
    Should you help Graham get more money to waste?

As care coordinator you will most likely have to deal with the utility companies (gas, electricity, water) if debts have accrued, and help the service user deal with these. Modern utility companies have pressed for all dealings to be dealt with through the Internet and web based tools. As a minimum they expect to deal with their customers by telephone. I remember one water company saying that they would not deal with postal information at all. Many service users with an enduring mental health problem do not own a computer, may not have computer skills and some do not even have a telephone.

There is clearly a gulf between what the utility companies offer and what some service users are able to deal with. As a care coordinator you will need to act as an advocate in these instances, or even as a translator. The language of the utility companies and large bureaucracies is not usually the everyday plain English that may be required and you will need to support service users in understanding what is needed.

In Graham's case a particular instance arose when dealing with a gas company, which would not accept his gas reading. He had signed up to transfer to a different gas company, but this was being blocked as they would not accept the gas reading. Many telephone calls over a six month period did not seem to solve the problem, as both gas companies were sending bills to be paid and threatening court action. The final straw came when in discussion with the gas company I suggested that they send out someone to read the gas meter. It seemed a simple solution. But the call centre operator responded with 'By law we do not have to send someone to read the meter.' I pointed out that however accurate this might be, it was not particularly helpful in moving things on. At this point the operator refused to speak to me as I was not the service user. I asked to speak to a manager, which was refused. I was getting a little wound up myself by this time. The operator stated that this telephone call was being recorded for monitoring, to which I responded that I was glad as perhaps someone with some common sense might get to deal with it. I think I also made some derogatory comment about their 'mission statement'.

If a professional with years of experience could get so frustrated, imagine how the service user would be expected to deal with this situation without support. Graham had no telephone, so we decided to write to the Gas Ombudsman to explain the predicament. Amazingly a situation which had dragged on for over six months, involving numerous telephone calls and letters to two different gas companies, was cleared up within a few weeks.

You may need to deal with agencies providing cleaning and domestic services or other care services. You will need to deal with the finances behind this, often involving justifying the case to a funding panel and organising the agency and contracts. The service will have to be monitored and funding renewed where appropriate. Increasingly service users are being encouraged to organise their domestic care for themselves through the use of direct payments or as part of the 'personalisation' agenda (HM Government 2007). In this case payment is made directly to the service user, who can then employ somebody of their own choice, a friend or a neighbour. This is a process that has been successfully adopted in other areas of disability but in general has so far been under-subscribed to by mental health service users. The care coordinator would have a role in monitoring the success of this process.

Housing is a key issue up and down the country and is of great importance to service users. Helping service users to access housing, writing letters of support and liaising with housing associations over non-payment of rent and disputes with neighbours may form part of the care coordinator's role.

> ## Activity 3.2 Critical reflection
>
> You may consider that it is not part of the mental health professional's role to deal with housing issues, benefits problems and debts to water companies. These used to be considered to be the realm of the social worker. What are your thoughts on this?
>
> To counter this argument I would point to reports that have highlighted the importance of housing and finance in maintaining good mental health (Mental Health and Social Exclusion 2004). In this respect it highlights that service users are firstly people, whose basic needs are the same as anyone else's. The mental health professional needs to think holistically when supporting people in the community. These are the issues which cause people stress and which, therefore, impact on their mental health. Graham has difficulty managing his money and runs up debts with his landlord. This has led to moves towards eviction. Under such stressors he may relapse and this could lead to an admission to hospital.

The above are just a few examples of where the care coordinator will be expected to liaise with outside agencies revolving around all aspects of the service user's life. The care coordinator is responsible for organizing these many agencies to work together, making referrals, signposting appropriately and chasing up services and reports. The care coordinator will be the key person, who will be expected to have knowledge relating to all the agencies involved. They will be the person any professional or outside agency will initially contact for information.

Role blurring

As can be gathered from the above the role of the care coordinator has become a generic role, being open to any suitably qualified mental health professional. It is not specific to a mental health nurse, social worker or occupational therapist. For this reason there has been some criticism of the role from the professional standpoint in that it appears to encourage a blurring of roles between the various professionals concerned (Brown et al. 2000). There has been concern that a loss of professional identity can lead to stress and burn-out (Brandon et al. 2003). Others have highlighted that the overlapping of roles can enhance team working (Burns 2004). This is part of an ongoing debate over the need for specialist versus generic roles in community mental health, which will no doubt continue into the future. I will not enter this debate here but when in practice you will be able to observe this yourself and perhaps come to your own conclusions.

It has been suggested that the particular relationship between nurses and doctors is different in the mental health setting to other settings (Fagin and Garelick 2004). The traditional role of the patriarchal doctor and the subordinate nurse has been seen to have substantially changed in mental health. The moves towards nurse prescribing powers and control over hospital admission, which may occur in crisis resolution and home treatment teams, highlight this change in relationship (Jones 2006).

Recovery

The model of practice adopted by modern mental health services is that of the Recovery Approach (National Institute for Mental Health in England 2005). The ethos of this is built into the care planning system. The process of assessment and review should revolve around the service user, who should be at the centre of the process. Their views should be sought and acknowledged at all stages. The care plan itself will be constructed in consultation with the service user, who is asked to sign the care plan along with the care coordinator to denote agreement.

The Recovery Model and the idea of a person centred approach are clearly closely linked. In general these are the principles which drive much of modern mental health policy. The use of the wellness recovery action plan (WRAP) is an integral part of forming the care plan. This was developed by Mary Ellen Copeland in the United States of America and has been adopted in the United Kingdom as part of the recovery process (Copeland 2011). The emphasis is on the service user developing their own plan based on their own experiences and needs rather than this process being led by the care coordinator or mental health services.

A typical WRAP would cover the following areas:

- things that keep me well;
- dealing with stress;
- reading and responding to the warning signs;
- crisis plan;
- getting back in control;
- environmental planning.

Also on this theme of self-determination is the use of advance directives. You may be aware of these from other areas of health such as older adults or people with life limiting or terminal illnesses. These can also be used by people with mental health problems in order to state their preferences if they become ill. It may state that they would prefer certain treatments or would not want other treatments, for example electro-convulsive therapy (ECT). As far as possible their wishes should be adhered to.

Person centred approach

> ## Activity 3.3   Critical reflection
>
> Consider your own standards of hygiene and values in regard to living standards. What are your standards of hygiene? How would you react when criticised?
>
> How would you deal with a situation in which the service user was 'happy' to live in housing conditions that are much lower than you can accept?
>
> Would you accept a cup of tea or coffee from them?
>
> How would you feel if a service user was determined to do something that you thought was a bad idea? How would you deal with this?

When visiting people in their own homes it is part of the mental health professional's role to take account of people's living conditions. These may reflect someone's mental health. If the person normally manages the household tasks and keeps a tidy house, then the house starts to become run down or cluttered, this could indicate their mental health is deteriorating and they are beginning to neglect themselves.

On the other hand the mental health professional needs to be self-aware enough not to impose their own standards upon others. We may all have different standards of cleanliness and we would all react quite badly if our standards were criticised. If people are mentally well, they are entitled to live by their own standards as long as they are not in breach of any environmental health laws. Many readers may have watched *Life of Grime* and you may come across similar situations. If the person is seen as mentally well to live in the community they can live by their own standards.

In the case of Graham, he had such a passion for recycling that he would not throw anything away. He bought *The Times* newspaper every day but never had time to read it, so he just stacked them on top of each other for later. The trouble is that later never came, so they were just piled up for years nearly to the ceiling. He also piled cardboard boxes up to the ceiling as when he had to leave his last address he did not have enough boxes for his packing. This had been a number of years earlier, so the living room was completely full with boxes and newspapers. The kitchen was piled high with tins of food or kitchen towel, which he had bought in bulk for economy. There was just a narrow 'corridor' to walk through the living room and kitchen made up of boxes, tins and newspapers. At times the 'corridor' itself became engulfed with used tissues. He would not throw them away on the grounds that they could be re-used or recycled. His motives were very laudable but he never got around to recycling anything, so the house became increasingly cluttered.

At one time the Environmental Health Officer was involved but said they could not intervene unless there were vermin or other pests. The interventions, therefore, became a series of intellectual negotiations in order to recycle newspapers, boxes, etc. For instance he did not want to throw the newspapers away on the grounds that he had not yet read them. This became a circular argument. Over a number of years progress was made but it had to be at his own pace and with his agreement.

I supported another service user who had lived on the streets and in hostels for over ten years. I supported him in getting a housing association flat and to get a grant to buy furniture. With this money I persuaded him to buy a secondhand cooker, which would be delivered over the weekend. On the Monday morning I had a telephone call from the secondhand shop saying that the man had contacted them and did not want the cooker but wanted his money back. I visited the service user, who said that he did not want anything secondhand and would prefer something smaller but brand new. The same applied to everything else he acquired. Despite being offered furniture, curtains and other household items for free he declined them and waited until he could save up to buy brand new. For many months all he had in his flat were carpets, a cooker and a bed. But he was happy with this. Gradually over the next year he acquired a sofa and a television.

I realised that I had tried to impose my own standards on this service user. I had assumed that he would be happy with secondhand items. I learned from this.

A salutary note can be made at this point to highlight a perennial tension that exists within mental health services. On the one hand the services are embracing the principles of the Recovery Model, person centred approach and service user involvement but on the other hand the service is the enforcer of the Mental Health Act (MHA). There is clearly a tension and possible conflict here, which is recognised by many service users and professionals alike.

Mental Health law

It is not appropriate to go into any detail here about the Mental Health Act 1983 (DH 2008) as it is a very large topic of its own. Certain aspects of the Mental Health Act are covered in other chapters. Nevertheless I will cover the specific elements that may fall under the responsibility of the care coordinator.

The amendments to the Mental Health Act in 2007 (Barber et al. 2009) incorporated elements of the move towards the Recovery Model and the recognition of service user involvement. The amendments recognised for the first time the right of a service user to have an advocate, in response to which advocacy services have sprung up all over the country (Bogg 2010).

The Mental Health Act (MHA) is the means by which the community and service users themselves are protected. Despite this view it can be seen by many individual service users as a weapon to be used against them and to cajole them into receiving treatment that they do not feel is necessary. Here lies an inbuilt tension and source of possible conflict.

The care coordinator must be able to embrace these potentially conflicting elements. In the first instance it may be the care coordinator who is requesting and initiating an assessment under the MHA. The care coordinator may have observed behaviour that has caused concern or they may have received reports from relatives, housing authorities or police that the person has been behaving in an unsafe manner. This may be either threatening harm to themselves or to others. If an MHA assessment is deemed necessary the care coordinator will play an integral role. This conflict between being person centred and enforcing the MHA can clearly place strain on any therapeutic relationship.

The care coordinator will be responsible for reporting back to the governing authorities in respect to other aspects of the MHA. For instance if the service user had been admitted to hospital on Section 3 of the MHA they may be placed on a community treatment order (CTO) when discharged from hospital (Griffith and Tengnah 2008).The purpose of this CTO would be to ensure that the service user cooperates with the treatment outlined in the care plan. Examples of what this would include could be:

- to take medication as prescribed;
- to engage with care coordinator and community mental health team;
- to attend appropriate out-patient appointments with consultant psychiatrist;
- to see the second opinion approved doctor (SOAD) as required within CTO.

If the above conditions are not met then the consultant psychiatrist can consider recalling the patient to hospital. Both the use of the MHA and the CTOs are regularly reviewed both by the local hospital managers and by the mental health tribunal system. The purpose of these reviews is to ensure that the treatment is correct and is in keeping with the MHA. The care coordinator will be expected to produce a report of social circumstances for these hearings. The service user may well be represented by a solicitor, an advocate or both at the above hearings. Care coordinators need to prepare themselves for being questioned on their reports. In the past this was a role which fell to the social worker but nowadays the care coordinator is seen as the most appropriate person.

Another element of the MHA that is particularly relevant for the care coordinator is the entitlement to 117 aftercare (Barber et al. 2009). This refers to a particular paragraph of the MHA which ensures aftercare to service users who have been taken into hospital under Section 3. The individual will have a statutory right to aftercare and the care coordinator will be the key person who will carry out this responsibility. An element of having 117 status is that appropriate care packages will be provided without any payment expected from the service user. This can become an important point when seeking funding for various elements of a care package.

Within the role of care coordinator will be a requirement to liaise with the approved mental health professional over aspects of the MHA (Brown et al. 2009). In the past this was primarily the role of social workers but since the amendments to the MHA in 2007 this role has been opened up to any suitably qualified mental health professional, which may include mental health nurses, occupational therapists and psychologists as well as social workers.

As an adjunct to knowledge about the MHA, mental health professionals in the community will need to have a knowledge and awareness of the Mental Capacity Act 2005 (Department for Constitutional Affairs 2007). Again aspects of this are dealt with in other chapters. The Mental Capacity Act requires the professional to make an assessment of an individual's capacity in regard to any necessary decision making. The main issues are that there should be a presumption of capacity unless there is evidence to the contrary and that any decisions made on behalf of the service user should be in that person's 'best interest'.

Communication

Key to all of the above is the core skill of communication (Hayes and Llewellyn 2010). The need for the care coordinator to liaise with so many different professionals and agencies requires good communication skills in all areas.

It is salutary to note that nurses and other professionals often rate their own communication skills very highly but that patients often report less satisfaction and maintain that communication could be improved (Bach and Grant 2009). Other surveys have highlighted that clients have felt themselves misunderstood and unsupported by their social worker (Koprowska 2010). The lessons to be learned are that communication is at least a two way system and that we can continually learn and improve.

First the care coordinator needs to be able to communicate effectively with the service user. This will involve the use of many interpersonal and informal counselling skills. These include listening and attending, empathy, information giving and support in the context of a therapeutic relationship (Bach and Grant 2009). Establishing a degree of rapport with the service user is essential to this therapeutic relationship. From the service user's perspective this is often seen as the most important aspect that contributes to a positive outcome of treatment. From the service user's point of view it does not seem to matter necessarily what professional background the person comes from, but more important is the level of rapport with that professional.

Clearly good communication skills are necessary for any professional working in mental health, whatever the setting, in an acute hospital or day hospital facility. But what is significantly different when working in the community is that you will be seeing people mainly in their own homes. Psychologically and practically this has a major impact on the relationship. As a professional you need to be aware that you are visiting the person on their own territory. When a service user is in hospital or visiting a community mental health centre they are aware that you are on your territory. The professional appears to hold the power and initiative. However friendly and inviting the centre may try to be, in general the service user is aware that it is your ground.

When you are visiting the person in their own home this is turned upside-down. It is you who has to knock and wait. It is you who has to be shown in and directed to a chair or sofa. The service user may offer you tea or coffee. They are subtly asserting their power and independence, which they may feel is not evident in hospital. If they do not want to see you they can refuse to answer the door or ask you to leave if they get upset. They have a perfect right to do this. You may have to contend with pet dogs or cats. This can be a problem if you have an allergy! Occasionally I have had to contend with uncontrolled and over-excited dogs leaping around the room while I am trying to complete an assessment.

At other times you may have to compete with the television, which is left on while you are visiting. In these circumstances you will need to utilise your assertiveness skills and politely ask the person to turn off the television or put the dog in another room. The professional also has to be aware of their own safety needs. You will be most often visiting service users as a lone worker. Prior to any visiting a risk assessment will need to be carried out and the professional should be aware of abiding by the lone worker policy of their employer. We will look at risk assessment in more depth a little later in this chapter.

On a local level good communication will be required within the multidisciplinary team. This will be both on a formal and informal level. This will involve team meetings, referral meetings, care planning and review meetings. Importantly it should also involve good supervision from the manager of the team. Most of the above will be based on good verbal communication. These will include the practice of assertiveness skills and good interpersonal skills. On a more formal level good communication requires good writing and reporting skills. Clinical notes will be required on a daily basis. At present these still take the form of handwritten notes but increasingly notes and reports are computer based. General computer literacy and wordprocessing skills are becoming an integral element of modern health services. Personally I feel that for the best use of clinicians' time there is a need for touch typing techniques to become a necessary skill. Otherwise valuable clinical time is taken up by producing computer generated reports using one finger typing.

When completing written notes you need to remember that these are legal documents and could be used in court or legal actions. As such they require accurate dating and signatures. The legal position is usually that if an action was not recorded, then it did not happen. The plea that someone forgot to write in the notes is not a very convincing defence in court. Report writing becomes a necessary skill. Reports may be required for all sorts of agencies apart from those specifically for mental health tribunals or for CPA reviews. These include reports to accompany housing applications, referrals for vocational support or assessment in regard to physical disability.

On a daily basis much contact is made by telephone in relation to liaison, referrals or general information gathering or sharing. A good telephone manner is, therefore, very important. It is essential to understand clearly what the other person is saying and equally to make sure that you are clearly understood. Important points and conversations would also need to be recorded in the clinical notes in order to ensure a written record.

Nowadays community workers will each have a mobile phone as well as an office landline contact. The mobile phone is useful for a number of different reasons. It clearly has a major use as part of ensuring safety among lone workers visiting service users in the community. It is a vital tool in allowing team members to be in regular contact with each other and to be able to telephone in to say that they are safe at the end of the working day. Each team will have its own lone working procedures in place and these will often involve the use of a mobile phone.

Another vital use of mobile phones is when you are with service users. A number of service users may not have a telephone of their own. Also most utility companies or the benefits agencies will not speak to a community mental health team member unless they have permission from the service user. It is extremely useful to be able to phone the appropriate agency and pass the telephone over to the service user sitting beside you. Following a few necessary security questions the agency involved will be happy to discuss the issues concerned. If you have to return to the office before speaking to the agency this process can become very protracted and disjointed.

The use of mobile phones enables community staff to remain out in the community for longer without having to return to the office to pick up messages or deal with enquiries. They can be dealt with while out and about, therefore speeding up the communication process. Clearly a note of safety needs to be added at this point to ensure that community staff comply with the law on the use of mobile phones while driving. Each employer will have its own policy on this.

Risk assessment

This section will focus on the issues which relate particularly to the community. In terms of risk assessment there are two distinct areas: the safety of the service user and the safety of you as a worker in the community.

The risk assessments used in the community are generally based on those produced by the Centre for Mental Health (Morgan 2000). These are well researched and based on established evidence. In general the main areas of a person's life are looked at in terms of diagnosis and past history. The risks associated are based on general evidence of a person's diagnosis and general life circumstances combined with specific individual experiences and history. The assessment looks at the following areas:

- suicidal risk;
  - risk of violence;
  - risk of self-neglect;
  - vulnerability to exploitation.

The risk factors cover the following range:

- gender;
- age;
- living alone, divorced, separated;
- unemployed/retired;

- diagnosis;
- history of past violence;
- history of suicidal ideas and attempts;
- family history;
- history of abuse, psychological, emotional, physical or sexual;
- history of self-neglect.

Regular reviews of the risk assessment are necessary in order to keep it up to date and to take account of recent events. Relating back to the theme of person centeredness there may well be areas of disagreement in putting together the risk assessment document. These should be discussed and documented.

The care coordinator should also take account of the idea of positive risk taking. We would accept that as adults we have the right to take certain risks in our own lives, whether they are physical, emotional or financial. Service users have these same rights. This concept of positive risk taking is built into the process of risk assessment. Mental health service users are allowed to take risks and make their own mistakes in the same way that we do. The qualifying comment needs to be added that this has to be within the bounds of the MHA as discussed earlier. This can clearly lead to a degree of tension and conflict.

Some of the issues of lone working have been mentioned above. This is one of the main differences between working in the hospital or day centre setting. In the community the normal practice is for professionals to be lone workers visiting people in their own homes. There are particular risks inherent in this. I have already mentioned the cultural difference in seeing people on their own territory. On top of this are the potential risks that exist because you are not in control of the environment. In a hospital emergency procedures are in place and other staff are available for support. In an office setting again emergency buzzers or alarms are common with other staff available. The furniture can be arranged so that you as a professional can easily access the exit, for example, your chair being nearest the door.

In someone else's house you do not have control over the layout of the furniture. You may have to sit where the person has indicated, even though your exit may be blocked. Some service users may even lock the door behind you as you enter. Depending on the service user this may be an acceptable practice or it may be quite intimidating for the visiting worker. The important point is that both the service user and the environment need to be risk assessed with regard to the community worker's safety beforehand. If the risk appears high, then measures need to be taken to reduce that risk. All community teams will have a system for workers to register the visits they will be going on and what time they will be expected back. This can range from a simple 'In/Out' board or book to more complex telephone call back systems. If the lone worker does not return or make contact on time, then pre-arranged safety checks can be followed. If a visit is assessed as potentially risky the service user could be invited to a local day centre or medical centre, where other staff would be available for support if needed. If this is not possible, then it may be necessary for the visit to be carried out by two members of staff. As mentioned above the use of mobile phones has greatly enhanced the safety aspects of working in the community, allowing for much more immediate communication.

I will share an anecdote concerning a service user for whom I was the care coordinator. He had a diagnosis of paranoid personality disorder. He sometimes believed that someone was following him near where he lived. He would, therefore, consider jumping them and beating them up before they got him. He was a regular user of alcohol and illicit drugs. He also had convictions for armed robbery. It was an easy decision to make not to visit him at his home, as there was no knowing what state of mind he might be in. So he was invited to be seen at the CMHT offices. When sober and not taking drugs he was a pleasant and affable young man. On one occasion he did not turn up for his appointment but phoned a few days later to ask if in future I could visit him at home, as that would be easier for him. I asked him why he had not been able to keep the appointment. He responded by saying that he had been 'out of his head' on various drugs. I pointed out to him that this was the exact reason I did not visit him at home. He acknowledged this and accepted it.

Care planning

First a thorough holistic assessment of the individual's needs will be required to inform the care plan. In order to make this assessment the following aspects must be taken into consideration:

- mental and physical health;
- treatment, including medication;
- contact with professionals and carers;
- social support;
- accommodation;
- finance and benefits;
- occupation and employment;
- leisure activities and interests.

The care plan will outline the care that will be offered to an individual (Hayes and Llewellyn 2010). It will explain what services will be offered and who will be responsible for carrying out the various actions. It will take into account any religious, cultural, gender and other requirements bearing in mind all diversity and equality issues.

Some care plans can be very straightforward in that all the needs can be met by one type of service. Sometimes this may all be provided by the care coordinator themselves. Others are more complex and will explain how to access help in an emergency and will include a crisis plan, which may help to prevent a hospital admission. Any disagreements will be recorded, as will any unmet needs. These unmet needs should go forward to inform managers and commissioners of services. The care plan is usually signed by both the care coordinator and the service user to ensure that the plan is mutually agreed. The service user is entitled to a copy of the care plan.

The information on the care plan will be available to be shared with other relevant professionals and clinicians on a 'need to know' basis. All information will be subject to the Data Protection Act (1998) and the service user will have access to information about themselves (Creek and Bullock 2008). In some instances service users do not wish to take part in the care plan process nor want a copy of the plan. This and the reasons behind it would need to be recorded.

Graham's case would be a more complex example. Read through the case study and complete Activity 3.4.

Case study – Graham (continued)

Graham has been referred following an admission to hospital. He has fallen into a state of self-neglect. He is in debt with his landlord and is being threatened with eviction. He has taken to drinking more and more alcohol recently and has hardly been eating. He is unemployed and living off benefits. His flat is in a very poor state; he has not cleaned it for months and it is full of clutter. He has not bothered to wash himself, shave, shower or wash his clothes for months. He has fallen out with his parents, who live nearby, and refuses to see them. He has become increasingly socially isolated. He has previously been on oral anti-psychotic medication but feeling that he no longer needed it he stopped taking it six months ago.

Activity 3.4   Critical reflection

Pick out the main issues and write these down in the form of needs of the service user, using the format: assessed needs; plans/goals; intervention; evaluation. These needs will drive your care plan. Try not to jump straight to interventions. Students can sometimes have a tendency to do this! The problem with this might be that you run the risk of overlooking certain needs, which will then not be addressed. In looking at the needs you will have to prioritise and look at what needs doing immediately and what will be part of an ongoing care plan. Then move on logically through planning, intervention and evaluation.

Compare yours to the care plan in Table 3.1.

Table 3.1 Care plan for Graham

Assessment	Planning	Implementation	Evaluation
1 Suitable accommodation	1 To remove threat of eviction 2 Graham to have secure accommodation	1 Graham to contact landlord to arrange payment and prevent eviction 2 Welfare benefits department or CAB to review benefits in order to ensure Graham is receiving all he is entitled to	Monthly care plan review including Informal feedback from Graham Feedback from Graham's parents Feedback from psychiatrist, GP and other professionals Health of the Nation Outcome Scale (HoNOS)
2 Be able to care for physical health needs	1 To reduce physical health care needs 2 Graham to become responsible for own physical health and to make appointment with GP for health check	1 Physical health check by GP 2 Support from care coordinator to develop budgeting skills and deal with debts 3 Support from community occupational therapist to become independent in activities of daily living	
3 Be able to care for mental health needs	1 To improve mental health symptoms 2 Graham to develop independent living skills 3 Graham to become independent in managing own medication	1 Education and monitoring from community mental health nurse regarding medication and self-administration	

(Continued)

Table 3.1 (*Continued*)

Assessment	Planning	Implementation	Evaluation
4 Social support	1 To develop supportive networks 2 Graham to combat social isolation 3 Graham to get involved with constructive activity 4 Graham to get involved with local community centre and develop interests and activities	1 Liaison with substance misuse team 2 Support from care coordinator to get involved in local community centre as a volunteer	
5 Education and support on how to cope with symptoms	1 To be able to identify and self-manage individual needs 2 Graham to access full entitlement of benefits and to develop budgeting skills 3 Graham to be responsible for own alcohol consumption and to develop techniques and support systems to control this	1 To develop crisis plan including knowing when – • to increase support from community mental health team; • to increase family support; • to review medication with psychiatrist; • to increase or change medication; • to involve crisis intervention team for intensive home support and treatment; • to consider admission to crisis house for short term respite and support; • to consider when admission to hospital is needed.	

Conclusion

This chapter has drawn upon the experience of a community mental health practitioner and discusses the main issues, needs and application of mental health care in the community setting. The chapter outlines what aspects of mental health care are the most concerning for clients and identifies that mental health symptoms may not be the main concern, although they are sure to contribute to the difficulties experienced by people living in the community with mental health problems.

However there is some indication that mental health symptoms can be exacerbated by the difficulties that all of us encounter living and working in a society that has developed its own rules on how we should all behave and to some extent think. Our values and behaviours therefore demonstrate our understanding of living within a society that can be made more evident in our care planning practices and interventions.

Community mental health practice therefore demands that a holistic approach is taken to empowering the client in becoming more independent and consequently more accepted by and within their local community. Community practitioners must also question their own values and behaviours in order for them to be become accepted too.

References

Bach, S. and Grant, A. (2009) *Communication and Interpersonal Skills for Nurses.* Exeter: Learning Matters.

Barber, P., Brown, R. and Martin, D. (2009) *Mental Health Law in England and Wales: A Guide for Mental Health Professionals.* Exeter: Learning Matters.

Bogg, D. (2010) The development of mental health law. In *Values and Ethics in Mental Health Practice.* Exeter: Learning Matters.

Brandon, T., Carpenter, J., Schneider, J. and Wooff, D. (2003) Working in multidisciplinary community mental health teams: the impact on social workers and health professionals of integrated mental health care. *British Journal of Social Work*, 33(8): 1081–103.

Brown, B., Crawford, P. and Darongkamas, J. (2000) Blurred roles and permeable boundaries: the experience of multidisciplinary working in community mental health. *Health & Social Care in the Community*, 8: 425–35.

Brown, R., Adshead, G. and Pollard, A. (2009) The importance of psychiatry and medication for Approved Mental Health Proffessionals. In *The Approved Mental Health Professional's Guide to Psychiatry and Medication.* Exeter: Learning Matters, pp. 1–5.

Burns, T. (2004) Community mental health teams. *Community Psychiatry 1*, 3(9): 11–14.

Care Programme Approach Association (2008) *The CPA and Care Standards Handbook.* Chesterfield: CPAA.

Copeland, M. (2011) *Mental Health Recovery and WRAP*. http://www.mentalhealthrecovery.com/aboutus.php (accessed 6 February 2012).

Creek, J. and Bullock, A. (2008) Planning and implementation. In J. Creek and L. Lougher (eds) *Occupational Therapy and Mental Health*. Philadelphia, PA: Elsevier.

Cronin-Davis, J. and Long, C. (2006) Tracking developments in mental health practice. In J. Cronin-Davis and C. Long (eds) *Occupational Therapy Evidence in Practice for Mental Health*. Oxford: Blackwell, pp. 1–11.

Department for Constitutional Affairs (2007) *Mental Capacity Act 2005 Code of Practice*. London: The Stationery Office.

DH (Department of Health) (2006) *Reviewing the Care Programme Approach: A Consultation Document*. London: Care Services Improvement Partnership.

DH (2008) *Reference Guide to the Mental Health Act 1983*. London: The Stationery Office.

Fagin, L. and Garelick, A. (2004) The doctor–nurse relationship. *Advances in Psychiatric Treatment*, 1: 277–86.

Griffith, R. and Tengnah, C. (2008) Mental health and the law. In *Law and Professional Issues in Nursing*. Exeter: Learning Matters, pp. 93–111.

Hayes, S. and Llewellyn, A. (2010) *The Care Process: Assessment, Implementation and Evaluation in Health and Social Care*. Exeter: Reflex Press Ltd.

HM Government (2007) *Putting People First: A Shared Vision and Commitment to the Transformation of Adult Social Care*. London: Department of Health.

Jones, A. (2006) Multi-disciplinary team working: collaboration and conflict. *International Journal of Clinical Nursing*, 15(1): 19–28.

Koprowska, J. (2010) What do we know about effective communication? In *Communication and Interpersonal Skills in Social Work*, 3rd edn. Exeter: Learning Matters.

Mental Health and Social Exclusion (2004) *Social Exclusion Unit Report*. London: Office of the Deputy Prime Minister.

Morgan, S. (2000) *Clinical Risk Management: A Clinical Tool and Practitioner Manual*. London: Sainsbury Centre for Mental Health.

National Mental Health Development Unit (2011) *Mental Health Services on Road to Recovery*. http://www.centreformentalhealth.org.uk/news/2011_mental_health_services_on_road_to_recovery.aspx (accessed 7 February 2012).

National Institute for Mental Health in England (2005) *Guiding Statement on Recovery*. London: Department of Health.

4 Care planning in acute mental health care

Maria Yuen

Learning outcomes

After reading this chapter you will be able to

- Recognise the care planning needs of a person suffering from acute mental health problems
- Identify the main issues when planning care in the acute setting
- Discuss the legal and ethical implications of care planning in acute mental health care
- Identify political influences upon care planning in mental health care

Introduction

The term 'acute mental health care' is used to describe the health interventions provided when an individual is experiencing acute symptoms or a mental health crisis. This chapter describes care planning for individuals with acute mental health care needs that have necessitated admission to an inpatient mental health unit. Acute care planning is part of a process of assessment, goal setting, intervention and evaluation. This process could be described as an 'acute care pathway'.

The case study of Steph will be used to illustrate the different aspects or acute care discussed.

Acute care is indicated for a person who is experiencing symptoms of mental ill health which have increased to a level where

- the person is in extreme distress and ability to function is disrupted;
- the person cannot be cared for within the place they are living;
- the person is posing a risk to themselves (such as suicidality) or to others (such as aggression towards others) due to their mental illness.

Mental health inpatient units

The main roles of mental health inpatient units are to provide a high standard of humane treatment and care in a safe and therapeutic setting for service users (DH 2002). Put simply this involves

- assessment of mental health needs;
- treatment of acute mental health symptoms;
- management and reduction of risk factors;
- discharge to appropriate place of accommodation and link in with services who will provide ongoing support.

Psychiatric intensive care units are small specialist units for people experiencing acute mental distress who require more intensive care than a regular acute mental health unit. These units would be appropriate for patients who are at high risk of suicide or patients who are likely to be physically aggressive or display very chaotic behaviour. Hence these units have a higher nurse to patient quota of staffing. They are also likely to have locked doors to restrict patients who may want to leave the ward (Beer et al. 2001).

Mental health crisis leading to hospital admission and application of the mental health law

A mental health crisis involves an individual experiencing acute distressing symptoms of mental illness, such as hallucinations or delusions. Mental illness is likely to have implications for those close to the individual, as well as social/financial factors. For instance, there could be increased stress on relationships due to a person's change in behaviour due to mental illness. Likewise, there would be financial implications if a person has not been able to manage their affairs adequately while unwell. A person may have deteriorated gradually over time, sometimes weeks or months. Other people relapse quickly, such as over the course of a week. It is realistic to expect a person who is newly admitted to an inpatient ward to be displaying florid or acute symptoms and possibly to be in mental distress. Although the containment of the ward and the support from health professionals can at most times be reassuring and certainly offer safety, the unfamiliar environment can also be anxiety provoking for others and cause more distress in the short term. A person's level of insight, or extent to which they acknowledge they are mentally unwell, will also greatly affect what is appropriate for their care plan.

The Mental Health Act is the law which governs the mental health treatment and detention of a person against their will, which might be relevant when a person lacks insight and when mental illness puts the person or others at risk. Where a client is detained in hospital, you will need to have an understanding of the relevant 'sections' of the Mental Health Act in order to plan care effectively. (See Chapter 1 for a list of main sections under the Mental Health Act.)

Crisis teams and care coordination

A care coordinator is a qualified mental health practitioner who has the responsibility of overseeing a person's mental health care under the Care Programme Approach (CPA) (Hardacre 2006). They will know the person's mental health and social history and work with the person over an extended period of time, possibly years. They would most often be working as part of community based services such as a community mental health team (CMHT). An individual's care coordinator would be able to help identify when the person is experiencing acute mental health symptoms and would then draw in support from other services, such as a crisis resolution team.

Crisis resolution teams were developed within mental health services in the UK following government guidance in the National Service Framework for Mental Health (DH 2004). The role of crisis teams is to intervene when an individual is in an acute mental health crisis. They tend to work short term with the aim of resolving the crisis by offering intensive support to individuals within their own homes. If a crisis cannot be resolved they would arrange for the person to be admitted to an acute mental health unit.

The acute inpatient environment

Gaining an understanding of both the physical and non-physical components of the inpatient environment will help greatly with practical care planning.

Physical components include the actual ward setting (the building, the bedrooms, furniture, equipment, etc.) and the people therein (clients, staff, visitors, etc.). Mental health inpatient units may be standalone buildings or part of a larger general hospital. They will have ward areas where clients sleep, eat and spend time during the day, as well as clinics and staff offices. They are also likely to include other resource areas which clients can access such as activity rooms, a gymnasium, cafes and garden or outdoor area. Mental health units need to be as safe as possible for clients and this will be evident in certain design features such as security codes for doors, and avoidance of ligature points in ward areas (i.e. structure points which could be used as a means for a person to hang themselves).

Wards can be very busy places populated with clients and an array of different health practitioners at any one time including nurses, healthcare assistants, doctors, occupational therapists, care coordinators, as well as visitors and volunteers. It is important to remember that wards can be quite overwhelming, alien environments for clients who are already dealing with acute mental health symptoms.

Nonphysical components of the mental health unit include rules, routines and group dynamics.

Mental health wards are by necessity run with rules and structure. Meal times, medication rounds, visiting times and therapy activities commonly form the basis for daily routine. Ward rounds and meetings with other practitioners also feature significantly as part of a typical week for clients. Understanding the typical routine on a ward and the physical environment will greatly enhance your ability to know how to organise care planning from a practical point of view. For instance, if a ward has quiet interview rooms these could be used for one-to-one talking interventions. Similarly, family meetings could be scheduled during visiting hours.

Wards are communal living spaces. An appreciation of group dynamics helps to enhance understanding of how people within a group environment influence each other's behaviour and emotions (Napier and Gershenfeld 1999). It is natural within shared living for bonds or relationships to form, for some individuals to clash socially and for small 'cliques' to form between those with some commonality. It is part of good ward management to consider these issues.

Therapeutic milieu

All physical and nonphysical components make up what can be termed the *therapeutic environment*. Therapeutic milieu is a term used similarly to refer to how the environment itself is used as an instrument for facilitating therapeutic benefits for the client (Kirby et al. 2004). There are many ways in which an inpatient ward, when viewed as a therapeutic milieu, can be altered or developed to help benefit clients. All the assessment and treatment ideas in this chapter are dependent on understanding and use of the therapeutic environment.

Working in a multidisciplinary team (MDT)

The team of staff on a ward may consist of the following:

- a ward manager
- staff nurses
- health care assistants
- occupational therapists
- domestic staff
- medical staff
- a ward clerk
- activity coordinators
- volunteers.

Other professionals who may also form part of the MDT are

- social workers
- care coordinators
- crisis resolution home treatment team staff
- clinical psychologists
- workers from other agencies relevant to the service users, e.g. advocacy, supported residential settings
- social services.

Communication between a potentially wide range of professionals who have different work bases can be extremely challenging. This is especially so in an acute setting where issues pertinent to a person's care can change rapidly and where adjustments to a care plan need to be known by all staff quickly in order to ensure safety, for example when a client's suicidality increases.

It is the responsibility of all team members to share information and to be aware of processes in place to ensure good communication. The most established ways of sharing information are through written or electronic documentation (e.g. clinical notes) and in MDT meetings. Effective MDT meetings allow for members to discuss a service user's progress, and collaboratively devise goals, including discharge plans. A well-functioning MDT can reduce the chance of a client being delayed in hospital due to bureaucratic processes, and therefore reduce pressure on services.

Other examples of commonly used strategies for sharing information in a timely and organised way are:

- one-to-one discussion with MDT colleagues;
- a diary or board for writing service users' appointments;
- daily handover on change of nursing shift;
- a board in the staff office showing current service users' names, room number and observation level.

Skills required to work within acute care

Working within a busy ward environment with acute unwell people can be hugely challenging as well as rewarding. Planning care within acute care requires a holistic, empathic view of the client. It involves excellent organization and communication skills to coordinate care within what can be quite complex systems and a myriad of other professionals within a multidisciplinary team. As there is often high pressure for clients to receive treatment and be discharged as quickly as possible, there is a need to work efficiently and often under pressure and to deadlines. The use of clinical supervision and peer support is essential to prevent burnout (Carson and Hollway 2008). Continuing professional development (CPD) is also necessary, especially to access specialist training.

Activity 4.1 Critical reflection

What could be the challenges of working with practitioners from a variety of different disciplines? How could you improve your understanding of the roles of other specialty disciplines?

Case study – Steph

Steph is a 56-year-old woman with a diagnosis of depression who has been known to mental health services since she was in her late 20s. She has had many previous hospital admissions.

She had been refusing to let her community psychiatric nurse (CPN) or staff from the crisis resolution home treatment team into her flat to visit her. There was evidence she had lost a lot of weight and had stopped taking her oral antidepressant medication.

The care team had concerns that she was at risk of neglecting herself and recommended that she required assessment for hospital admission. After the appropriate assessments were made, she was admitted to hospital under Section 2 of the Mental Health Act.

Assessment within acute care

The purpose of assessment is to gather information about a client and then to determine their *needs,* based on the problems they are experiencing. The following are a range of assessment tools which may be used.

Interview

An assessment interview with the client is conducted in the first day or so after admission by a consultant psychiatrist, with a staff nurse and possibly a junior doctor also present. The aim of the interview is to determine the client's mental state, gather background information and to begin setting care planning goals. See the Appendix for an overview of the Mental State Examination (MSE).

An initial interview should also cover questions about the following (Norman and Ryrie 2004):

- the client's perception of circumstances leading to admission and their view about being in hospital;
- any treatments or services which the client is engaged with at the moment;
- living circumstances;
- social supports and family situation, including if the person has any dependents;
- history of mental illness and family history of mental illness;
- current daily activities including interests;
- employment history;
- financial situation;

- outstanding stressors in the person's life and how they are coping with them;
- the client's expectations of being in hospital.

Interviewing has a vital role in establishing rapport with the client and beginning to work in partnership towards the client's recovery. This is no mean feat, however, considering the client is acutely unwell. You need to be empathic, a good listener, able to sensitively ask difficult questions and remember (or quickly write down) lots of complex information. You also need to be realistic about the extent to which a client is willing or able to engage in a formal interview. They might be affected by poor concentration, poor insight into their mental health problems, anger at being in hospital, or be responding to hallucinations, to give just a few examples. In these circumstances, a flexible approach is recommended, for example having several shorter interviews.

Similarly, it is necessary to use clinical reasoning to build a realistic picture of a client, when their self-report may not be literally, factually accurate. For instance, if a client has a grandiose delusion about painting priceless works of art (and it is clear this is not actually true), this suggests the person may have to spend their time painting and that this is important to them. It does however build an accurate picture of their financial situation. Therefore you should always consider information from interviews alongside what is already known about the client, i.e. information gleaned from the client's medical file and collateral history from people who know the client well, such as family or the care coordinator.

Separate assessment interviews may be conducted by different members of the multidisciplinary team, who may need to find out more in-depth information on a specific area. For example, a social worker would ask more specific questions about housing needs and financial circumstances.

Activity 4.2 Critical reflection

How would you seek to build rapport with someone who is acutely unwell and didn't want to speak to you? For instance, a person who is very depressed? Or someone who is floridly psychotic?

Physical examination

A physical examination is conducted by a doctor on admission as standard procedure. It examines the client's cardiovascular, respiratory and nervous systems which may indicate further physical tests that need to be conducted, for example an x ray or blood tests.

Medical and nursing staff have a prominent role in assessing and monitoring a client's physical health while they are in hospital. There is evidence that people with a history of mental health have high prevalence physical health problems (Thangavelu et al. 2010). Be mindful also that the implications of experiencing acute mental illness symptoms, such as low mood and motivation, can lead directly to physical health issues, such as poor nutrition and diabetes.

Observation

Observation is a key assessment skill within the acute setting, which is used by all members of the MDT. As clients' behaviour and symptoms may change so rapidly within the acute phase of illness, observation is one way to effectively assess the client in an unobtrusive way. Good observation involves more than merely 'looking' at what is happening. It involves

1   observing details (noticing the different aspects of the person/situation);
2   understanding the context (what is the background information? What are the social and cultural and organizational considerations which influence what is being observed?);
3   interpreting what has been observed using clinical reasoning (what is the meaning of what I can see? How could it be described in a professional, objective way?).

Good observation can give you an excellent assessment of a person's mental state and ability to function, at that particular time.

During observational assessment examples of what you should take note of are:

- **Appearance** Does the client appear to have washed or groomed themselves recently? Are they wearing clean clothes which are appropriate for the weather and setting?
- **Physical health and mobility** Do they have any obvious physical health issues? Does the client appear under or over weight? What can you notice about the health of their eyes and skin? Can they mobilise independently? Do they use a walking aid?
- **Behaviour** What do you observe the client spending their time on in hospital (e.g. sitting, pacing, sleeping)? How do they behave in different everyday situations such as during social interaction? How would you describe their general level of motor activity (e.g. settled or restless?). Are they able to perform daily living activities such as eating, bathing, shopping?
- **Cognitions** Does the person appear oriented to time, place and person? Are they able to concentrate and pay attention to a task or do they look distracted? Are they able to problem solve (such as work out what to do when faced with an unfamiliar situation) and how do they deal with frustration?
- **Social interaction** How well does the person interact with others? Are they aware of social cues and norms? Do they initiate social contact? What do you notice about the person's verbal and nonverbal communication skills?

Observation has the advantage of being able to be utilised as an assessment tool in situations where the client is unwilling or unable to engage in interview or more structured assessment modalities. For instance, a person who is severely depressed and almost mute may be unable to tell you they lack motivation, but observing the person lying in bed all day and not attending to his/her own self care is good evidence to note this as your assessment.

Formal observation levels are used within ward environments, which give guidelines on how often a client should be observed. Level 3 Observations, for instance, mean a client must be constantly observed and hence always in the company of a member of ward staff.

Structured assessments and formal assessments

Formal or standardised assessment tools are those with set guidelines on how to administer them and interpret the results. They have been developed through the use of research and may take the form of questionnaires, checklists, interviews or observed tasks. Some advantages of using standardised assessment are as follows:

- Some are able to be used as outcome measures to reflect a change in the client over time.
- They have researched validity and reliability.
- They are already written and have instruction manuals, hence avoiding the need to develop your own tools.

Some disadvantages of using standardised assessments are:

- They can be time consuming to use.
- It can be difficult to stick to instructions/rules for administering assessments when clients are unpredictable in their behaviour and mental state, which affects the validity of the results.
- It can be expensive to purchase the tools. Some also require special training to learn to administer them, which comes at further cost.

Examples of standardised assessments used within the mental health field are:

- Beck Depression Inventory: self report questionnaire to assess severity and presence of symptoms of depression (Beck et al. 1988);
- Psychotic Symptom Rating Scale (PsyRATS): a rating scale to assess dimensions of hallucinations and delusions (Drake et al. 2007);
- Liverpool University Neuroleptic Side Effects Rating Scale (LUNSERS): a self-rating scale to assess medication induced side effects (Day et al. 1995).

Family/carer assessment

Families, carers and significant others who know the client well can give key information to help contribute to the assessment process for the client. They are able to give details about the person's history and possibly the circumstances prior to admission. They are also often excellent assessors of how well a client has recovered during the course of the admission. Another way of describing this, is assessing to what extent the client is back to their 'usual self'. Hence they can be very helpful during the discharge planning process.

Family or carer assessment involves examining how the client's experience of mental illness has also had an impact on these significant people. Family/carer assessment involves investigating:

- How is the family/carer coping with looking after or being around the client? Are there any issues of stress or burnout or impact on relationships?
- Does the family/carer require more education about general mental health issues or the mental health service?
- Does the family/carer require more support (practical or emotional) to care for the client?

It is important to note that if family/carer assessments involve talking about the experiences and perspectives of the family/carer and not giving away any information about the client, then consent from the client is not required. If the family/carer asked for more information about the client or the client's care plan, you would need to seek consent from the client to discuss this.

Risk assessment

'Risk' is defined as 'a situation involving exposure danger; a possibility of harm or damage' (Oxford University Press 2011).

Understanding and assessing risk is an essential skill in mental health care. Risk factors can be considered broadly in categories of:

- *Risk to self* This includes suicide, self-harming behaviours, self-neglect, exploitation, physical/medical risks.
- *Risk to others* This includes aggression and violence.

Risk assessment involves considering the prominence of *risk factors* for the client. For instance, risk factors which are associated with suicide include:

- having a major psychiatric diagnosis, such as bipolar affective disorder or schizophrenia;
- having a family history of suicide;
- expressing suicidal ideas;
- misuse of drugs or alcohol;
- expressing hopelessness;
- previous suicide attempts.

(Morgan and Wetherall 2004)

Both a client's current and previous risk should be considered (Morgan and Wetherall 2004). Risk assessments must be formally documented.

Be mindful that the ward environment can have its own inherent risks for certain individuals. For instance, a client who is at risk of exploitation due to being sexually disinhibited during a manic episode could be at greater risk when admitted to a mixed gender ward.

Risk assessments need to be regularly repeated to reflect the changes to a client's mental state and circumstances during the course of admission. Within acute care, a new risk assessment is also indicated where the context or physical environment introduces different risks that need to be considered. Examples are when a team member takes a client on a home visit alone, during therapeutic activities involving sharps, and when travelling in a vehicle with a client.

Doyle (1999; in Kirby et al. 2004) identifies seven key questions to ask when assessing risk:

1   What is the likelihood of harm occurring?
2   How often is it likely to occur?
3   What possible outcomes may there be?
4   Who is at risk?
5   What is the immediacy of the risk?
6   What is the timescale for assessment?
7   What are the circumstances that are likely to increase or decrease the risk?

Realistically, all clients will have some dimension of risk in their presentation, as this is inherently linked to acute mental illness which requires hospitalization. While risk assessment can be an area fraught with anxiety, especially for novice practitioners, it is impossible to eliminate risk entirely. Good risk management will be able to balance therapeutic gain while still aiming for a safe outcome. A skilled clinician will be able to utilise positive risk taking to create opportunities for a client to recover. Positive risk taking should acknowledge risk but facilitate a positive, hopeful approach (Morgan and Wetherall 2004). An example within acute care would be allowing a client who has previously attempted suicide, but whose suicidality has reduced, to spend time at home alone.

Case study – Steph

Assessments conducted with Steph:

Observations: Nursing staff on the ward notice Steph is reluctant to speak to anyone and makes little eye contact. Steph appears guarded and suspicious when staff try to talk to her. She is spending all her time in her bedroom, refusing to come out for meals. Steph appears very thin and gaunt and wears the same clothes every day.

Interview: Steph was reluctant to speak to nurses or a doctor for more than a few minutes. She did report that she lives on her own. She has never been married and does not have children. She has a cousin who lives close by. She said that she does not want to be in hospital and is angry at having been admitted.

Steph's care coordinator reported that Steph had not been taking her antidepressant medication regularly over the last three months. She did not appear to be washing and was often in her pyjamas all day. She had stopped leaving the house and it was noted on one occasion that food that had been bought for her was left untouched on the kitchen bench for days.

Steph's cousin rang the ward and told the staff that she had noticed Steph stopped calling her about a month ago and had been very suspicious and irritable.

Risk assessment: The main risk for Steph is self-neglect when she becomes unwell. She assaulted staff during an earlier hospital admission, which was also during an episode of depression.

Intervention

The following are brief descriptions of a range of the interventions which may be available within acute care.

Medication

Pharmacological treatments have arguably the strongest evidence as efficacious intervention within acute mental health care. Advances in medication have transformed the potential for recovery from acute mental health symptoms as well as long term maintenance of mental health.

It is beyond the scope of this book to detail all the medications which are currently most widely used within mental health care. The following are the broad categories of drugs mostly used:

- **antipsychotics** – to alleviate psychosis;
- **antidepressants** – to reduce depression;
- **anxiolytics** – to reduce anxiety;
- **mood stabilisers** – to treat mood disorders, such as bipolar affective disorder;
- **antiparkinsonian agents** – to manage the side effects (called extrapyramidal symptoms) which can be a side effect of taking some antipsychotic medication.

A consultant psychiatrist has the responsibility for prescribing and reviewing pharmacological treatments, while nurses play a key role in administration and monitoring concordance (also referred to as compliance) and side effects. All members of the care team should have a general knowledge of drug treatments and side effects and know where to seek further advice if required.

The National Institute for Clinical Excellence (NICE) is a body which sets standards within the UK for treatment of different health conditions, including guidance for prescribing medication for specific conditions. Drug treatments are used within acute mental health care for both short term management of symptoms (such as sedatives used to alleviate agitation with a person who is depressed) as well as medium to longer term relapse prevention. It is usually necessary to review a person's drug treatments during an acute episode, as part of the care planning process. The ward environment can be helpful as a place where the client can be constantly monitored by qualified staff for adverse side effects of medication.

Electroconvulsive therapy

Electroconvulsive therapy (ECT) has historically been seen as a controversial treatment since its development in the 1930s. The National Institute for Clinical Excellence (2003) gives guidance for the use of ECT only for people experiencing severe depression, catatonia (a syndrome associated with schizophrenia and mood disorders, where the person's movement is affected to be in either a state of stupor or extreme overactivity). ECT involves the client having electrodes put on the head and an electric current passed through the electrodes to cause a seizure. ECT is always administered with a general anaesthetic and a muscle relaxant (which prevents body spasms). ECT is recommended for use for short term treatment only, in situations which are life threatening and/or where other treatments have been tried and unsuccessful. For instance, where a severely depressed person might be unable to speak, eat or drink. A prominent side effect can be short term memory loss (Barker 2003). ECT is frequently used in conjunction with other treatments, which are appropriate for longer term use.

Psychological therapies

These interventions consist of a number of approaches know as talking therapies and are usually carried out by qualified psychologists or psychotherapists. Talking therapies are recommended with government policy as being available to all people who need mental health services but there are still problems with being able to gain access. Consequently talking therapies include a wide range of verbal interventions including the main ones which follow:

- cognitive behaviour therapy (CBT)
- solution focused therapy
- brief therapy
- dialectic behaviour therapy (DBT).

Psycho education may also fall into this category as people will need information and advice from knowledgeable professionals who can advise about side effects and self-management skills. All interventions however should lead to a personalised approach to care planning.

Psychosocial interventions (PSI)

Psychosocial interventions are a range of treatments using psychological principles which aim to help a client experiencing psychosis manage symptoms more effectively (Gamble and Curthoys 2004)

The main features of psychosocial interventions include:

- developing *formulations* following assessment, to understand the client's problems;
- an emphasis on coping strategy enhancement and problem solving, to manage symptoms. Examples of coping strategies for hearing voices might be listening to music through earphones or wearing earplugs (Nelson 1997);
- use of cognitive behavioural therapy (CBT) strategies;
- family assessment and intervention. PSI takes on a theory that family dynamics, especially families who are described as 'high expressed emotion' can contribute to chances of an individual relapsing. Thus, intervention which focuses on stress management, education and communication training (Reader 2002).

Wellness recovery action planning

Wellness recovery action planning (WRAP) (Copeland 2005) is a tool to develop an individualised system for identifying self-management strategies. WRAP applies principles of a recovery model which strongly advocates for empowerment, improving wellbeing and self-responsibility. The tool includes sections such as 'Wellness tools', 'Daily maintenance plan' and 'Crisis plan'. Wellness tools are considered to be any strategies which enhance wellbeing, especially those which are easily accessible and which the client knows works for them, such as exercise, seeing friends, keeping a diary, attending support groups or eating healthily. WRAP is a tool that could be introduced to clients during admission and used to encourage self-management and to prevent relapse.

Emergency interventions

The following interventions could be utilised in critical and emergency clinical situations posing immediate and significant risk to the client or others.

- *De-escalation* describes communication techniques used to diffuse a potentially risky situation, such as a client who is threatening aggression or violence. De-escalation is the first and arguably most important skill to utilise in emergency situations to prevent harm. Muir-Cochrane (2003) gives strategies for de-escalation which include being respectful, encouraging the patient to talk and elicit their point of view, maintaining a large personal space and not arguing with the patient.

- *Seclusion* involves the client being confined to a secure room. Rationale for seclusion might be for the client to be in a low stimulus environment and to reduce risk of harm to others. This is an intervention which should be considered only in emergencies. A client placed in seclusion will be monitored very closely and alternative treatments initiated as soon as possible.
- *Restraint* involves physical handling of the client by staff in order to manage an emergency situation, such as violence towards others. Restraint requires specialist training which is regularly updated, and is only ever used as a 'team' (never performed by just one practitioner). Restraint techniques enable staff to keep the client in recognised 'holds' and then to move them to a place of safety (Polczyk-Przybyla and Morahan 2001).
- *Rapid tranquillization* In some circumstances, administration of emergency medication will also be necessary to allay acute symptoms which are increasing risk. An example is administration of antipsychotic medication to counteract agitated and aggressive behaviour in a client who is responding to auditory hallucinations.

All emergency interventions have potential to cause distress to staff and clients alike. It is important that supervision and debriefing are used to support those involved.

Making links with family and carers

Stevenson (2003) highlights that the client can lose a sense of connectedness with others when admitted to hospital. Hence, making links with family and carers has benefits for the client in terms of helping them to maintain relationships and a sense of belonging to their social world.

We can support the client to keep in touch with family and friends by making visiting hours clear, ensuring a safe and appropriate place for visits with children and facilitating access to a phone, as just a few examples.

Families and carers may also play a key role in the care planning process. Stevenson (2003) describes considerations when working with families, including different means of communication such as letters and meetings. He also highlights communication techniques to help facilitate effective, open relationships with families, such as use of narrative interviewing and reflection. Mitchell, Stanbury and Arnold (2004) similarly recommend care team members learn skills in how to engage with families effectively. They go on to describe aspects of the care planning in which families and carers should be included, such as psychoeducation, interviews and illness management strategies.

The vital support that families and carers often provide can also expediate discharge for the client and again help facilitate sustainable recovery. Families and carers can provide feedback, alongside the client's own perspective, on the client's mental state through the different stages of treatment. They may also provide practical support with the aim of enabling the client to return to normal activities, such as accompanying the client on home visits.

Families and carers should have the option to have their own 'assessment' whereby they have the opportunity to discuss how they are coping themselves with caring for the acutely unwell person, and any support they might feel they need for themselves. Referral onto more specific carer support groups might be indicated.

Family therapy is a more specialised form of intervention in which family (or carer) is directly participating in the treatment process alongside the client. There is good evidence that focused family work is effective in helping a person recovering from psychosis and preventing relapse. Gamble and Curthoys (2004) hence advocate strongly for health workers to prioritise training and time for this work.

Occupational therapy

Occupational therapy is concerned with how a person's occupations (activities) are affected by illness or disease. Occupational therapists must therefore encourage people to develop their skills in everyday tasks in a creative and therapeutic way.

Occupational therapists are frequently part of a multidisciplinary care team. Occupational therapy assessments give information on a person's abilities to perform daily living activities, with reference to a person's motor, process and social skills and the person's environment. This information is useful for the whole care team in understanding how a person functions and support that is required after discharge from hospital. Occupational therapy treatment might involve group or individual sessions with a focus on restoring and developing the client's skills in meaningful occupations, such as self-care, domestic tasks or leisure activities.

Therapeutic activity

Clients residing in inpatient units need a range of activities to help structure the day, aid recovery and occupy time meaningfully. Boredom has long been seen as having a negative impact on mental health and is potentially an issue within ward environments.

Star Wards (Janner 2006) is a document written by Marion Janner who personally had experience of mental health inpatient units as a client. The document, which gives 75 ideas for activities and strategies to improve the hospital experience for clients, has received much publicity nationally. Ideas presented in *Star Wards* include:

- access to gym, library, spiritual care and computer facilities;
- walking groups, men's and women's groups;
- daily programme of activities to be planned;
- TV, DVDs and board games made available on every ward.

Therapeutic activities might take place on the ward, in community settings or in other facilities within the hospital setting, such as a gym or garden. Volunteers and activity coordinators can also be recruited to help run activities.

All staff can play a role in promoting the benefits of getting involved in a range of activities. Engaging in simple interest activities that are within the client's interests and capabilities is also a way of 'normalizing' the hospital experience for the client and allows opportunity for making choices and taking responsibility.

Discharge planning

A goal for all clients admitted to a ward is to improve sufficiently to be discharged to a safe place, where they will be able to continue their recovery. Effective discharge planning involves cohesive and transparent multidisciplinary team working, and close communication with the client and carers/family. Often a meeting will be called to ensure an organised process for discharge. Be aware that some practical aspects of discharge planning, such as finding alternative accommodation, can take enormous amounts of time causing further stress for the client and a drain on acute services. Where possible, they should be organised as far in advance as possible.

Discharge planning is a process which involves identifying:

- the client's current views on discharge;
- evaluating current interventions and planning future treatment;
- where the client will live when discharged;
- the plan of how the client will be supported after discharge – e.g. family, care coordinator, support workers;
- a management plan in the case of relapse after discharge.

Interventions which could be part of the discharge planning process include:

- referral to other professionals for specialist assessment or treatment, e.g. a clinical psychologist;
- identifying alternative accommodation that better meets the clients' needs; this might involve support from a social worker;
- meetings with family and carers to discuss concerns and support needs;
- applying for funding for a package of care such as regular support workers or home help;
- liaison/advocacy with the clients' employers;
- identifying financial issues, including access to benefits if relevant;
- referral to support services and resources that will aid recovery and quality of life, such as support groups and day centres.

Recording acute care plans

How care plans are recorded will depend largely on your area of practice. As with all documentation, this should be done in a timely way. This is all the more relevant in acute care, where a client's mental state, and hence care needs, can change rapidly. Increasingly, care plans are written using electronic record keeping systems. Care plans may be described as *integrated,* where all health professionals of different disciplines contribute to the same care plan. An advantage of this is that it puts the client 'at the centre of care'.

The client will require specific goals for the acute care admission, even though they are likely to already have a care plan pertaining to their care in the community. The acute care plan should focus on goals that are relevant to the acute episode.

One effective method of writing goals on a care plan is using the acronym SMART. This method dictates that goals are written to be Specific, Measurable, Achievable, Realistic and Timely (Lloyd 2010). Within acute care, it can be difficult to gauge what is considered a 'realistic' or 'achievable' goal and how long to allow for a goal to be achieved. Some clients can be so changeable in presentation, it can feel like a struggle to get an accurate assessment, let alone set goals. Below are some common challenges to care planning within acute mental health care:

- It is difficult to determine timelines for intervention as all individuals take different amounts of time to recover.
- Clients don't recover in a linear fashion. They may deteriorate before improving.
- It can be difficult to know baseline level of functioning, or what a client is like when they are well, in order to set realistic goals.
- There may be pressure from hospital managers for clients to be discharged as soon as possible to free up bed space for other patients.
- Other realistic issue which may be barriers to the care you would like to provide are: resources available, staffing levels, your own skills and the time you have to implement the care plan.

Some strategies for managing these challenges are:

- Set smaller short term goals while the client is in hospital. These might be daily or weekly goals.
- Revisit the goals regularly. Expect to have to adapt and modify goals as a client's situation changes.
- If a client has had previous hospital admissions and/or acute episodes of mental ill health, use what has been learned from these experiences to help set realistic goals. For instance, what has helped on previous occasions to speed recovery? How long did it take the client to recover last time? Many clients have a 'pattern' of relapse.
- Speak to people who know the client well such as family or a care coordinator, about what the person is like when they are well.
- Communicate regularly with the multidisciplinary team.
- Be aware of the community based supports available to the client, such as community support workers, care coordinator. Consider how your care plan can link in with this community support to ensure seamless care for the client.

- Be realistic about your own capacity when committing to involvement in goals with a client. Also be aware of the resources at your disposal for providing care. For instance if you know that you can only see the client twice a week then your care plan needs to reflect what can be achieved within this timeframe. If you know that a colleague who is working on a similar goal with your client can also see them once a week, then you could coordinate your work and raise expectations of what can be achieved.

Setting care plan goals collaboratively

Client-centred care planning means the client's needs and perspectives are taken as a priority when planning care. It also means the client has involvement in decision making and is given choices and responsibilities as part of the care plan. All of these ideas are consistent with an empowerment model (Kirby et al. 2004; Lloyd 2010).

The traditional medical model, with its 'doctor knows best' philosophy, has been previously criticised as placing patients in the role of passive recipients of care. However, working with an empowerment model brings up its own ethical dilemmas and ambiguities. While few health professionals would argue that clients shouldn't be involved in their own care planning, in reality there are degrees to which this might be debated to be safe, ethical or practical. Some of these issues are made even more complex in acute care. Some examples of challenging questions which arise on the topic of working collaboratively with the client and families/carers are:

- How can someone who is out of touch with reality (such as someone with psychosis) make reasonable decisions about their care?
- How can someone who is detained in hospital on a Mental Health Act section 'collaborate' in their care plan when they don't want to be in hospital in the first place and don't agree that they are unwell?
- How can a client be expected to understand the complexities of their diagnosis/their treatment/mental health services in order to make informed decisions?
- What about clients who have cognitive problems, such as learning difficulties?

The Mental Capacity Act 2005 provides the legal guidance 'for acting and making decisions on behalf of individuals who lack the mental capacity to make particular decisions for themselves' (Department for Constitutional Affairs 2007: 15). It is important to have an understanding of this framework, in order to ensure clients can make decisions for themselves as much as possible and to help protect people who lack the mental capacity to do so. The Act would assist with how you make decisions on some of the ethical questions above.

Under the Mental Capacity Act, a person is presumed to be able to make their own decisions 'unless all practical steps to help him (or her) to make a decision have been taken without success' (p. 19). A person is assessed for capacity for each particular situation requiring decision making and may, therefore, have different capacity depending on the context of the situation. For instance, a person may have the capacity to choose where they want to live when given a number of choices, but would not have the capacity to be able to find a property and arrange to live in it. Incapacity is not based on the ability to make a wise or sensible decision.

Even the client who lacks insight can be involved in their own care and should not be denied these opportunities. It also does not mean that these clients would be resistant to, or not be able to benefit from, having therapeutic relationships and rapport with you as a practitioner.

Good communication is essential to collaborative working and you must make time for it. Some forums for allowing formalised communication include care planning meetings, meetings with the family/carers, meetings between professionals, and individual meetings with the client.

Below are some strategies and considerations for working collaboratively on care planning:

- Involve the client in aspects of their care plan, taking into consideration safety and practicality within the hospital setting. If a client is suicidal and is under nursing observation, for instance, they might not be allowed to leave the ward on their own, but they could be given options of activities to do within the ward. They could also be told in advance at what time staff can go on an escorted walk with them.
- Consider that even being able to make small day to day choices can help a person to maintain some sense of self-esteem, self-identity and feelings of being valued.
- Be aware of legal restrictions if a person is detained under the Mental Health Act and how this might have implications for the care plan. For example, a client on Mental Health Act Section 2 or 3 would require a consultant psychiatrist to approve and sign Section 17 leave forms before they would be allowed leave off hospital grounds.
- Provide information so clients and families/carers can make informed choices. Examples of relevant information are: treatment options, visiting times, how to access money, and rights of the client. People have different preferences for how they best take on board information, so have a variety of different mediums available. Examples might be verbal information, links to websites, leaflets or notice boards.
- Use your rapport building and listening skills. Even if the client has limited or no insight into their mental health issues there is usually some point of commonality, which they can share with you as an empathic practitioner. For instance, a situation may arise where a client detained under the Mental Health Act insists on wanting to be at home. As a practitioner you think he is mentally unwell and needs treatment. However, you can acknowledge that being in hospital is causing the client distress, and you both have a

common wish for the client to not be in hospital anymore. You could use this as the basis for setting short term goals around coping with the anger and frustration and for working towards a discharge plan.

An advanced directive is a document written by a person when they are mentally capable, to detail how they would like certain aspects of their care to be managed, in case of a relapse. For example, they might include descriptions of treatments they would prefer, or how they want personal affairs to be managed for them if they have to be admitted to hospital. Advanced directives can assist practitioners with being client centred. The Mental Health Act however may still be used to treat an individual without their consent. 'The *Triangle of Care*' is a document published by the National Mental Health Development Unit (2009) which advocates for carers to be an essential part of care planning within acute care. It is a reminder that carers' views need to be included for goal setting.

Activity 4.3   Critical reflection

How would you set goals with a person who shows no insight and does not believe they require care?

How would you explain what a care plan is to someone who lacks insight?

Evaluation of the care plan

Care plans should be regularly and frequently reviewed as it is likely a client's mental health during an acute episode will change significantly. Updates should be made when there are new goals and when current goals are achieved or need modifying. The care plan should be evaluated as part of regular MDT meetings. The information discussed within this chapter and identified from our case study, Steph, will be used to create a sample care plan in the acute mental health setting using the APIE framework (Lloyd 2010).

Conclusion

This chapter explores the planning of care for a person who is suffering from acute mental health symptoms. Because of the nature of their symptoms people who are acutely ill may not always believe that they have any problems or that other people do not want to harm them but help them to cope with such distressing symptoms.

The challenges facing a practitioner in this environment are therefore many; however, in carefully assessing both the needs of the individual person and the strange environment in which they find themselves, the mental health

Table 4.1. Care plan for Steph

Assessment	Planning	Implementation	Evaluation
1 Reduce symptoms of depression and improve mood	Review medication and reinstate antidepressant	1 Doctor to prescribe medication 2 Discuss different forms of administration to improve concordance 3 Monitor side effects	Daily monitoring from nursing staff, weekly with consultant psychiatrist
2 Improve and monitor physical health	Assess physical health. Increase weight to healthy range. Establish healthy eating habits. Establish healthy sleep patterns	1 Refer to dietician 2 Encourage regular meals 3 Monitor intake and exercise 4 provide information on healthy living	Weekly monitoring as part of MDT meeting
3 To establish therapeutic rapport	To establish therapeutic relationship in order to plan care	1 Short frequent contacts to establish rapport 2 Identfiy interests and values 3 Explain rights under MHA 4 Set short term goals for motivation, e.g. go to shop	Daily monitoring from nursing staff, weekly with consultant psychiatrist
4 To improve self-care	To complete washing and dressing independently. To improve motivation for self-care	1 Assess self-care abilities 2 Ensure adequate supplies 3 Encourage daily routine 4 Provide encouragement 5 Link with incentives	Daily monitoring from nursing staff, weekly with consultant psychiatrist
5 To develop self-management skills	To develop an understanding of depression	1 Provide education 2 Discuss coping strategies 3 Discuss WRAP	Daily monitoring from nursing staff, weekly with consultant psychiatrist
6 To engage in meaningful activity	To improve social networks and meaningful activity	1 Develop rapport 2 Identfiy interests 3 Provide information on opportunities available 4 Refer to occupational therapy 5 Set daily goal of 1 activity 6 Provide support and encouragement	Daily monitoring from nursing staff, weekly with consultant psychiatrist
7 To be discharged to accommodation that supports needs	Assess current support needs	1 Meetings with Steph, family and MDT to discuss current and future support needs 2 Investigate avenues for Steph to receive support after discharge, if this is indicated, e.g. regular visits from a support worker or even consider a change of accommodation if required	Review at MDT meetings

practitioner can help address their concerns and identify ways in which the client can become more involved in their care.

Working and being in the acute care environment can appear to be very different from being in other settings within mental health care and the constant observation and evaluation of risk is never very far from the minds of practitioners. However this chapter has demonstrated that within such an unusual environment in which the client might find themselves willingly or not, it is still possible to develop a therapeutic relationship that is warm, collaborative and sensitive to the needs of individual clients.

Developing such a therapeutic relationship cannot only help the person to recover quicker but it can also be the practitioner's main tool in planning personalised mental health care.

References

Barker, P. (ed.) (2003) *Psychiatric and Mental Health Nursing*. London: Arnold.

Beck, A., Epstein, N. and Steer, R. (1998) An inventory for measuring clinical anxiety: psychometric properties. *Journal of Consulting and Clinical Psychology*, 56(6): 893–7.

Beer, M.D., Perieira, S.M. and Paton, C. (2001) Psychiatric intensive care: development and definition. In M.D. Beer, S.M. Pereira and C. Paton (eds) *Psychiatric Intensive Care*. London: Greenwich Medical Media Limited, pp. 1–11.

Carson, J. and Holloway, F. (2008) Understanding and managing stress. In D. Bhugra and O. Howes (eds) *Handbook for Psychiatric Trainees*. London: RCPsych Publications, pp. 157–68.

Copeland, M. (2005) *Wellness Recovery Action Planning*. Liverpool: Sefton Recovery Group.

Day, J.C., Wood, G., Dewey, M. and Bentall, R.P. (1995) A self rating scale for measuring neuroleptic side effects: validation in a group of schizophrenic patients. *British Journal of Psychiatry*, 166(5): 650–3.

Department for Constitutional Affairs (2007) *Mental Capacity Act 2005 Code of Practice*. London: TSO.

DH (Department of Health) (2002) *Mental Health Policy Implementation Guide: Adult Acute Inpatient Care*. London: HMSO.

DH (2004) *The National Service Framework for Mental Health: Five Years On*. London: TSO.

Drake, R., Haddock, G., Tarrier, N., Bentall, R. and Lewis, S. (2007) The Psychotic Symptom Rating Scales (PSYRATS): their usefulness and properties in first episode psychosis. *Schizophrenia Research*, 89(1): 119–22.

Duncan, E.A. (2002) *Foundations for Practice in Occupational Therapy*. Edinburgh: Elsevier.

Gamble, C. and Curthoys, J. (2004) *Psychosocial interventions*. In I. Norman and I. Ryrie (eds) *The Art and Science of Mental Health Nursing: A Textbook of Principles and Practice*. Maidenhead: Open University Press.

Hardacre, K. (2007) *Care Programme Approach: Care Coordination, Core Functions and Competencies*. London: Department of Health.

Kirby, S.D., Mitchell, G., Cross, D. and Hart, D.A. (eds) (2004) *Mental Health Nursing: Competencies for Practice*. New York: Palgrave Macmillan.

Janner, M. (2006) *Star Wards: Practical Ideas for Improving the Daily Experiences and Treatment Outcomes of Acute Mental Health In-patients*. London: Bright.

Lloyd, M. (2010) *A Practical Guide to Care Planning in Health and Social Care*. Maidenhead: Open University Press.

Mitchell, G., Stanbury, C. and Arnold, S. (2004) Acute in-patient setting. In S.D. Kirby, G. Mitchell, D. Cross and D.A. Hart (eds) *Mental Health Nursing: Competencies for Practice*. New York: Palgrave Macmillan.

Morgan, S. and Wetherall, A. (2004) Assessing and managing risk. In I. Norman and I. Ryrie (eds) *The Art and Science of Mental Health Nursing: A Textbook of Principles and Practice*. Maidenhead: Open University Press.

Muir-Cochrane, E.C. (2003) The person who is aggressive or violent. In *Psychiatric and Mental Health Nursing: The Craft of Caring*. London: Arnold.

Napier, R.W. and Gershenfeld, M.K. (1999) *Groups: Theory and Experience*. Boston, MA: Houghton Mifflin Company.

National Mental Health Development Unit (2009) *Triangle of Care Carers Included: A Guide to Best Practice in Acute Mental Health*. London: National Mental Health Development Unit.

Norman, I. and Ryrie, I. (eds) (2004) *The Art and Science of Mental Health Nursing: A Textbook of Principles and Practice*. Maidenhead: Open University Press.

Oxford University Press (2011) *Oxford Dictionaries*. Available at http://oxforddictionaries.com/definition/risk (accessed 27 October 2011).

Polczyk-Przybyla, M. and Morahan, T. (2001) The use of restraint. In M.D. Beer, S.M. Pereira and C. Paton (eds) *Psychiatric Intensive Care*. London: Greenwich Medical Media Limited, pp. 158–68.

Reader, D. (2002) Working with families. In N. Harris, S. Williams and T. Bradshaw (eds) *Psychosocial Interventions for People with Schizophrenia: A Guide for Health Workers*. New York: Palgrave Macmillan.

Stevenson, C. (2003) Family support. In P. Barker (ed.) *Psychiatric and Mental Health Nursing*. London: Arnold.

Thangavelu, K., Muraleedharan, V. and Hampson, M. (2010) Recognising serious physical illness in the acutely unwell psychiatric patient. *Journal of Psychiatric Intensive Care*, 6(1): 47–56.

5 Child and adolescent mental health

Marjorie Lloyd and Alison Owen Traynor

Learning outcomes

After reading this chapter you will be able to

- Identify the main challenges facing child and adolescent mental health
- Identify the main resources to help children and adolescents with mental health problems
- Identify and discuss treatment options for children and adolescents
- Plan care for a young person with mental health needs

Introduction

Children's mental health needs is a relatively new area of mental health practice only because in the past there was a general belief that developing minds and brains would naturally go through many emotional and perceptual changes. Identifying abnormal behaviour and thoughts was therefore far more difficult as children were learning how to develop into an adult who could live independently and make their own decisions. Learning from our mistakes is perhaps the most common form of development in children where parents carefully allow the child more and more freedom to make mistakes so that they can learn from them. Discovery learning is also a common method of allowing children to work out for themselves how to approach a problem, whether that is in mathematics or sport, so long as there is someone there to guide them along the correct path. In a 2008 review of services for young children with mental health problems it was identified that a multiprofessional approach was necessary in order to ensure that young people received the best care available:

> We all play a part in helping children and young people grow up. Mental health and psychological well-being are not the preserve of one profession or another, or of one government department or another.
> Children and young people need to be supported by professionals who help each other out and by a truly joint approach that is child- and family-centred, from the Government at national level as well.

Anyone in contact with a child has an impact on that child's mental health and psychological well-being. The challenge for all of us is to remember that and to be able to respond if things start to go wrong.

(Davisdon 2008: 6)

It is perhaps therefore the fields of education, sociology and psychology where much of the research has been carried out that provide us with an evidence base for normal behaviour in children. There are many well-known experiments (that would not be allowed to be carried out now) involving children and young animals' responses to parenting, learning and emotional development. This chapter will therefore explore some of the original work around children's mental health development before identifying areas of practice that can be developed into a care plan.

The developing child

Maughan (2011) suggests that child development can be viewed as a number of interconnecting systems within the child's life, including parents, friends, school, siblings, community and culture, all meeting to provide the best available care for that child. Such systems may be natural or material but together they can help form a strong resilience to everyday life so that development and maturity can take place. Children in general develop both physically and mentally by attaining developmental milestones. These are stages in their development that can be observed and measured, for example, learning to walk and speak. While it is recognised that not every child will develop at exactly the same time there are time frames within which a child should develop their skills and maturity. Influences upon child development are widely researched and recognised within the social and psychological fields of practice including cultural, social and spiritual and systems theory. Child development is therefore a very complex but natural event in which all children can expect to achieve some level of independence by the time they reach adulthood. The sequence shown in Table 5.1 is very familiar in the child development literature as having identified such stages of psychosocial development throughout the lifespan. Taking a lifelong approach to child development helps us to see that where perhaps a child has been unable to go through a stage successfully, say because of trauma or illness, that they may need to revisit that stage later in their life.

Barriers to effective child development

For some children there are events in their lives that they will have no control over that may slow down or even stop their development all together. Some of the barriers include:

- **Conflict and famine** A child living in this environment may not have enough to eat so that their bodies can grow and/or their education may be affected or stopped altogether.

Table 5.1 Erikson's stages of psychosocial development

0–18 months Trust vs Mistrust	Babies learn how to explore themselves and the world around them. They begin to develop their own character or ego and they often explore with their mouths as this is the most developed part of their body at this stage.
18 months–3 yrs Autonomy vs Shame	Children grow and develop at a fast pace during this stage. They learn to walk and talk and their coordination develops. Self-esteem develops as we learn to control our bodies, e.g. toileting. The 'terrible 2s' learn to become more confident or vulnerable if they begin to experience shame that affects their self-esteem.
3–5 years Initiative vs Guilt	Children become more independent and they start being more creative with their imagination, e.g. imaginary friends and are constantly asking 'why'. However if their goals become frustrated they may begin to experience guilt because they are unable to meet their own needs or the needs of others.
6–12 years Industry vs Inferiority	Children spend more time in school and away from their carers. They are learning quickly about the world around them but also about their relationships with others. If such relationships are damaging they can affect the child's self-esteem and lead them to feeling inferior.
12–18 years Identity vs Role	During this period children become adolescents and begin to learn about themselves in more depth. Their ego develops and it can appear like they are going through the terrible 2s all over again. They compare themselves with others in order to shape their own identity and can therefore be vulnerable to role confusion and identity confusion.
18–35 years Intimacy and Solidarity vs Isolation	This stage is about being a young adult where we learn to strengthen relationships and develop our identities into a more solid role with responsibilities. Intimacy is developed within our relationships but if not successful, isolation can occur where we find making relationships with others difficult.
35–65 years Generativity vs Self Absorption or Stagnation	This stage is known as middle adulthood where we focus on our work and on developing a strong basis for our lives. It is dependent upon all the previous stages being navigated successfully so that we can call upon our peers and relationships with others to support us in this very productive stage. Without such support we can stagnate and not be able to move on.
65 years Death Integrity vs Despair	This stage is where we reflect upon our lives and develop a sense of integrity that we have achieved all that we were capable of achieving. Alternatively we may experience despair and a sense of loss for what we never had or were unable to achieve. Consequently this last stage is also dependent upon how successful we were at previous stages and we may return to some of the those stages to try and work through them again, e.g. Identity vs Role.

Source: Adapted from Pressley and McCormack (2007).

- **Poverty** Children's bodies needs enough food as well as the right amount of different foods in order for healthy muscles, organs and skin to grow. Without enough food and shelter children can quickly become malnourished and at risk from disease and harm if unaddressed.
- **Lack of nurturing** Children need love and warmth from other human beings in order to develop self-confidence and self-esteem. This is best provided in a loving family environment but may be disrupted when parents become ill, families split up or they move away from the extended family and grandparents to seek work or affordable housing, etc.
- **Lack of socializing** Many of the above barriers to effective child development include social activities that are important for children to learn how to be part of a local community. Each local community will have its own rules and beliefs that everyone must adhere to in order to be accepted. Sometimes this is achieved by children attending local clubs or after school activities.
- **Lack of education** All children have a right to education but for various reasons not all children can get it. Some of those reasons have been outlined above but there are other more subtle effects on the education of children that can be ignored. Children need to have access to education including transport, clothing (uniform), equipment and other resources such as books and pencils. Access to a local library can contribute greatly to a child's education as can time spent playing sports and learning about nature and the environment. Many of the needs of children however can only be met by adults who have the knowledge and resources to help the child to learn and to grow.
- **Inadequate housing** As well as a place where children are most often provided with food and safety a house is where the child can rest and learn. If housing is inadequate then the child will not be able to concentrate or sleep, both of which are essential for emotional and physical growth.

Jane-Lopis and Anderson (2007) suggest that mental health promotion within Europe now makes attempts to address childhood development as a preventative measure in children who may eventually develop a mental illness. The loss of parenting and nurturance can lead to an increase in depression and suicidality. They go on to suggest however that programmes in schools that attempt to encourage resilience in school aged children using cognitive and behavioural approaches have proved to be successful in preventing mental health problems in the short and long term.

Case study – Harry

Harry lives in a flat in a large town with his parents and two younger sisters. Harry is 10 years old and both his parents work hard to make sure he has enough food and clothing even though he is growing fast. Harry will be moving up to high school in the next year and will need to be prepared for helping him to cope with the change from being one of the oldest in the school to one of the youngest again. His parents are worried that he will get in with the wrong crowd and start taking drugs.

Activity 5.1

What would you suggest to Harry and his parents to help him cope with the change he is about to face? Would you choose any of the following? If not, why not?

- suggest that Harry makes friends quickly so that he will have support in his new school;
- buy Harry loads of books on becoming an adolescent;
- help Harry identify his own resources that will support him and buy him whatever he needs or asks for;
- go with Harry to the school open day, talk to the teachers and find out what resources are available to Harry and can be provided within his local community.

From the above scenario it becomes clear that there are many options Harry and his parents might choose; any and all of them may be of some help. The important thing to remember is that all children are also people in progress and that they have rights and opinions that must be respected. Taking a person centred approach to Harry's needs therefore is a practical and realistic way of helping him to grow and develop and become confident in his own abilities. In order to take a person centred approach we must be able to communicate and listen to what a person's needs might be. With children this may be quite different from communication with adults. Butts and Rich (2005) suggest that there is a 1 in 5 chance of children developing a mental illness and therefore it is important for professionals to be able to understand and recognise the signs. This requires good communication skills and some understanding of child development in order to identify when problems occur. Children and Adolescent Mental Health Services (CAMHS) therefore may be accessed on a number of levels or tiers which is an attempt to keep children in familiar surroundings for as much as possible. The tiers or levels are split into four areas of service delivery:

- **Tier 1**: primary care which includes all those services provided by the local doctor as well as teachers, nurses and social workers that the child may come into daily contact with;

- **Tier 2**: specialist mental health workers including psychologists, community mental health workers and specialist teachers and social workers;
- **Tier 3**: team services offered by a specialist CAMHS multidisciplinary team including psychiatrists, psychologists, family therapy workers, etc.
- **Tier 4**: very specialist services which include the rare but necessary acute care units or hospitals and secure provision for the management of risk and safety.

Holyoake (2005) describes the tiered system as ubiquitous, which suggests that it is not very easy to define in practice. However this may be because it is recognised that there should be the least disruption to children's lives and their development and so people who are already familiar with them should try to intervene in the first instance. If they are unsuccessful in improving the problem then they should refer to the next tier or level of services and so on.

Activity 5.2   Critical reflection: mental health services for children

Can you identify how you would access the CAMHS team in your local community?

Who would you contact first?

How would you explain to a child that they might need help from CAMHS?

Learning to communicate with children and adolescents

Children communicate their needs differently to adults, however children who do not learn to communicate their needs as children will probably have difficulty doing so when they are adults too. Communication is such a basic skill that we often take it for granted. However learning to communicate effectively may be affected by all of the barriers to child development identified above. When we communicate with children (and adults) we may fail to recognise the signs that there may have been barriers to their emotional and physical development.

The most basic communication skill with children is known as bonding or attachment theory and was identified in research by Bowlby (1969, cited in Vick and Nicolas 2005) who researched separation anxiety in infants. Bowlby concluded that it was very important for children to have nurturing relationships in order for them to develop and function within society. Much work has since been developed within social and psychological fields that encourage bonding relationships and the development of trust. Erikson's stages of development (see Table 5.1) identified a number of stages throughout the lifespan that people needed to achieve an acceptable level of functioning at, which could prevent mental health problems developing in later life. Current mental health policy in England (Department of Health 2009, 2011) argues that mental health problems can be prevented if we can develop resilience and strengths as children and adults in order to help us cope with challenges in future living. Such resilience can be developed within schools, families and primary and secondary health and social care in order to recognise and treat mental health problems quickly so that dependency upon services is not created at a young age and then continues throughout adulthood. In creating dependency upon health and social care agencies we not only prevent the young person from developing physically, sociologically and psychologically but also prevent their development of hope and recovery from mental health problems. Communicating with children who may develop mental health problems requires a subtle approach that does not pick them out or isolate them from their local networks of support. The following ways of providing information and education in order to develop resilience may be used.

- Go into local schools or community groups and give talks/provide information on mental health and wellbeing.
- Obtain information leaflets and distribute them to groups and schools.
- Develop relationships with local groups so that you become part of the group and are not seen as an outsider and can be trusted.
- Learn about local youth culture but do not attempt to use their language; you will probably embarrass yourself by getting it wrong.
- Monitor activity on social networking sites and encourage/role model open but safe communication.
- Develop local activities for children to meet up and develop supportive relationships if not available.
- Work closely with local doctors, nurses, health visitors, social workers, school nurses and youth services if you think there may be problems developing. Good interdisciplinary communication is essential in keeping children and young people safe.
- Learn about suicide prevention strategies in your local area and make sure others know about them too.

Vulnerable groups of children and young people

Children are already vulnerable if they do not have the coping skills or resilience to address their mental health needs. However there are additional vulnerabilities placed on children that are not always recognised. In a review of services the Department of Health (2008) identified the following groups of children who may find themselves more vulnerable than others:

- children and young people with behavioural, emotional and social difficulties;

- children and young people with learning difficulties and disabilities;
- children and young people with special educational needs (SEN);
- children and young people with life-threatening conditions (such as cancer);
- children and young people with chronic illness (such as diabetes);
- children and young people with physical disabilities;
- children and young people with specific genetic conditions (such as neurofibromatosis);
- children and young people with sensory disorders (such as those who are deaf);
- children and young people with autistic spectrum disorder;
- children and young people with other communication difficulties;
- children and young people with Down's syndrome;
- children and young people in care;
- children and young people at risk of suicide;
- children and young people who are being abused;
- children and young people who misuse substances or whose parents/carers misuse substances;
- children and young people who have been bereaved;
- children and young people in contact with the youth justice system;
- children and young people who are lesbian, gay, bisexual or transgender;
- children and young people from black and minority ethnic groups;
- children and young people experiencing housing difficulties;
- children and young people seeking asylum;
- young people not in education, training or employment;
- young carers;
- young runaways.

Children and adolescent mental health services

The Royal College of Psychiatrists (RCP 2010) suggest that children can be referred to CAMHS by their local doctor, social worker, school nurse or special educational needs coordinator (SENCO) if there is a problem identified that a child may need specialist help with. However in reality the people who work in CAMHS can be found in a variety of places including clinics, schools, youth offending services, day patient or inpatient services. The RCP (2010) go on to suggest that a child psychiatrist working with the CAMHS team will assess any problems and prescribe medication if necessary to help treat the problem. However other specialist services might become more involved including mental health nurses, psychologists and social workers who will work with children while they are living at home in helping them to address their needs.

The influence of law and policy on children's mental health

Feat (2005) suggests that children fall within a number of laws and polices around their physical and mental wellbeing which can cause some confusion for practitioners. In mental health law children can be detained under the Mental Health Act 1983 (amended 2007) for assessment (Section 2) and treatment (Section 3) and are also therefore entitled to aftercare (Section 117) and the legal support to protect their rights. Furthermore the Children's Act (1989) can make provision for removing the young person to a place of safety and/or secure environment (Section 25). However the use of law in children's services needs to take into account many factors that would need to be considered in context. These may include

- the wishes of the child and the risks these may present;
- the wishes of close family and the ability to provide safe accommodation;
- the need to keep families together while a young person is developing both mentally and physically;
- the ability of the parents to take care of the young person;
- the availability of services and accommodation.

In a study of the frequency and use of law in CAMHS, Mears et al. (2003: 8–9) found the following results:

- Where detention is formal rather than informal, psychiatrists almost exclusively use the Mental Health Act rather than Section 25 of the Children Act to detain young people with mental health problems.
- Detained patients tend to be older, with a substantial number aged 18 years or over.
- Detained patients are more likely to have schizophrenia or personality disorder than informal patients, who are more likely to have eating or mood disorders. Detained patients have greater psychosocial complexity.
- Consent obtained for treatment tends to be verbal rather than written.
- Psychiatrists' knowledge of the Children Act and consent issues is lower than for the Mental Health Act.

The report recommended the following:

- The specific needs of young people should be considered in the new Mental Health Act. This should include clarification of the primacy of consent (parental and patient) for young people.
- There is a need for training for health and social care staff in the use of the Mental Health Act, the Children Act, and in issues of consent. There may be particular value in joint training.
- There is a need to address the issue of the apparent low level of psychiatrists' training in mental health law.

- The consideration of CAMHS in the National Service Framework for children should address issues of consent, including the use of parental consent for the detention and treatment of young people on CAMHS in-patient units.
- The range of agencies providing services for young people with mental health problems need to review and resolve the discontinuities in care that result from different services having different age based criteria.
- There is a need for better liaison between CAMHS and adult mental health. Particular areas needing to be addressed include determining responsibility for admission for young people requiring formal admission, transferring care between services, and providing input for young people detained on general adult psychiatric wards.
- NICE should produce guidelines on the use of medication and other treatment for young people with mental health problems. These should also address the use of rapid tranquillization in in-patient services.
- In-patient services must recognise the importance of obtaining informed and continuing consent.
- Services should be encouraged to avoid verbal and blanket consent.
- Further research is needed into admissions under parental or local authority consent, and the choice between parental consent, child consent and the use of the Mental Health Act.
- Further research is required into how young people from ethnic minorities interact with in-patient CAMHS.

As with all laws relating to health and social care Codes of Practice are available to help practitioners interpret the law and apply it to practise safely and ethically. When working with children it is important to ensure that you are familiar with your legal and ethical obligations and are accountable to the child and professional and legal bodies for your actions. Consulting with colleagues in the multidisciplinary team is a necessity when working with complex areas of practice, not only for up to date information but also for your professional support and supervision. Chapter 36 of the *Code of Practice Mental Health Act 1983* (Department of Health 2008: 327) states that:

> The legal framework governing the admission to hospital and treatment of children is complex, and it is important to remember a number of factors. Those responsible for the care of children and young people in hospital should be familiar with other relevant legislation, including the Children Acts 1989 and 2004, Mental Capacity Act 2005 (MCA), Family Law Reform Act 1969, Human Rights Act 1998 and the United Nations Convention on the Rights of the Child, as well as relevant case law, common law principles and relevant codes of practice.

When considering whether the child or young person is able to consent to their treatment and care plan the Mental Capacity Act (2005) is not usually used but the general rule of the Gillick competence is used instead. This rule was created following a mother's appeal against her daughter seeking treatment from her doctor without the mother's knowledge. The Gillick competence is provided in the Code of Practice (DH 2008) as a guide to helping young persons consent to treatment.

> In the case of Gillick, the court held that children who have sufficient understanding and intelligence to enable them to understand fully what is involved in a proposed intervention will also have the competence to consent to that intervention. This is sometimes described as being 'Gillick competent'. A child may be Gillick competent to consent to admission to hospital, medical treatment, research or any other activity that requires their consent.
> ... The concept of Gillick competence is said to reflect the child's increasing development to maturity. The understanding required for different interventions will vary considerably. A child may have the competence to consent to some interventions but not others. The child's competence to consent should be assessed carefully in relation to each decision that needs to be made.
>
> (p. 337)

It is important therefore to remember that consent and consent forms should not be used as a blanket approach to care planning and interventions. All interventions should be discussed with the young person to ensure that they are happy to consent to them going ahead and if not that they be removed from the care plan.

Identifying mental health needs in a young person

Young people and children may present their needs in different ways to adults particularly if they already have difficulties with communication or relationship development skills. Such difficulties may be a natural part of their growing up and should be recognised and included when trying to assess a young person's needs (Limmerick 2006). They may also be an indicator that a young person is struggling to cope with life's demands.

Activity 5.3   Critical reflection: child/infant bonding

Go to the website of retired mental health nurse Felicity Stockwell (http://www .felicitystockwell.com/) and read her accounts of child/infant bonding in more depth. Felicity gives a detailed account of how the bio-psychosocial needs of children can result in some quite severe mental health problems. How could you address these issues?

Assessing physical health needs

All young people develop physically at different rates but within a given time frame. In adolescence in particular, puberty and growth spurts may indicate that the young person is more mature than they actually are physically or emotionally. Young people are naturally curious and will want to experiment with all sorts of activities. It is important therefore that they get the right amount of information for their needs in order to keep them safe from harm. Because their bodies are still developing, the correct diet, rest and exercise are also very important and can lead to mental health problems if not addressed, e.g. poor concentration, low mood and fatigue.

Assessing psychological health needs

As suggested above young people may give the appearance of being more mature than they actually feel inside. Their self-esteem may be very fragile and weakened quite easily by thoughtless remarks or suggestions. Identifying psychological needs is more difficult than identifying physical needs and good communication skills are important in being able to help the young person identify how they are feeling. This might be achieved by carrying out an activity together while chatting so that the conversation and/or relationship becomes less intense.

Assessing spiritual, social and cultural needs

Young people are heavily influenced by their local culture/community because they have an inherent need to fit in. This means that some children might go to extreme measures in order to be liked and accepted by their peers. Joining gangs or groups is the most common form of acceptance and they may appear to reject family members at this time. However family support is even more important at this time as a place of safety and support. Observing behaviour in a social setting can expose relationship development problems both with peers and families but must be addressed in order to ensure that the child feels safe and supported.

Assessing risks in children

Although there may be many obvious risks to children including poor diet, poor education and poor levels of support it is their psychological safety that may often be overlooked. This may be because the child is unable to communicate their needs, they may put on a brave face or they may feel that they have no one to talk to. There will be signs however that may or may not be observed in their behaviour that might help the professional identify that the child might need help (see the mental state examination in the Appendix). Signs might include all or some of the following but should be discussed with others if there is any concern.

- changes in patterns of living, e.g. eating, sleeping, going out, studying, self-care, etc.;

- withdrawal from groups and activities previously enjoyed;
- lack of communication or increased communication around unremarkable subjects;
- lack of emotion or over-emotional responses to everyday events;
- support networks disappear – friends no longer call or visit;
- lack of interest in things they used to enjoy, e.g. films, music;
- obsessional or ritualistic behaviour such as washing hands frequently, sorting items;
- aggression and outbursts of anger;
- constant tearfulness and crying;
- unusual hoarding behaviour – making collections of things, e.g. pens, knives, cigarette lighters;
- unusual grooming behaviour, e.g. excessive washing.

Behaviour is a significant way in which children and young people communicate with adults but is not intended to disguise their feelings; it may be the only way they know how to communicate. Sensitive observation and questioning may help the young person to discuss their feelings – perhaps for the first time – with someone they respect and trust. Relationships, although they may be difficult, are therefore a very important part of resilience and support for young people. It may be worth practising how you might approach a sensitive topic with a young person first, as it may be your only chance and if it goes wrong, trust and self-esteem will consequently again need to be built up.

Interventions to help children address their mental health needs

Cobb (2006) suggests that there may be a number of interventions to help children address their mental health needs in a supportive and effective approach. These include:

- counselling
- behavioural interventions
- cognitive behavioural interventions
- motivational interviewing
- solution focused therapy
- family therapy
- parental training
- child psychotherapy
- individual play therapy
- creative therapies
- group therapy
- pharmacology
- intensive care
- multisystemic therapy.

The list is quite extensive and no one person is likely to be greatly experienced in all of them. It is important to find out what is available to help children and young people so that their care plan can reflect what is available locally and how other professionals can help the young person develop coping skills and resilience.

The context of care planning for young people

Care planning for young people who have mental health needs can take place in various settings. We have already outlined the CAMHS framework for assessment and care planning that is recommended within policy guidelines. However in order for personalised care planning to take place the context within which the child is situated is very important for the care plan's effectiveness. Holyoake (2005) suggests that there are various ways that the context can influence the young person's care plan to ensure that it is effective:

- The family will need to be considered and where possible included in the care plan.
- The environment(s) in which the care plan is to take place will need to be considered and whether there are enough resources and support.
- The system within which the young person spends a majority of their time will need to be considered and how supportive it can realistically be, e.g. family, school, hospital, residential home, etc.
- The signs that the young person shows in needing support may be behavioural or psychological or both but they may not be able to communicate their needs verbally.
- Professionals and/or family may not be able to offer the support needed and other systems may need to be considered.
- Professionals must be aware of their own responses both verbally and behaviourally in developing a trusting relationship.
- Interventions should be visible, e.g. behavioural, so that everyone can see improvement and resilience.

Considering care planning for young people is perhaps one of the most complex areas of mental health practice, therefore consideration needs to be given to the person, their environment or context and the systems within which they live.

Activity 5.4   Critical reflection: complex systems in young people's mental health care

Take some time to think about how many systems a young person in your area of practice might encounter. Make a list so that it can be used as a reference point when planning personalised care.

Case study – Jack

Jack is a 16-year-old school boy who presents at the GP surgery complaining of abdominal pain and headaches which have been increasing in frequency and severity over the last three weeks. He is accompanied by his mother who is worried about Jack's reduced appetite and the fact that he has not been sleeping as well as usual. Jack's mother has also heard from school that he has been missing occasional lessons and there are concerns from school staff as Jack, who is a promising pupil, will be sitting his GCSE exams in four months.

In the above scenario Jack is identified as needing mental health support. The following care plan (Table 5.2) outlines some of the areas Jack may need help with. Depending upon who begins this process the care plan will need to address all of his needs and ensure that an holistic approach is taken to meeting them. While there is little information provided above, in reality we might need to ask

Table 5.2 Care plan for Jack

Assessment	Planning	Implementation	Evaluation
1 Jack is experiencing physical symptoms of pain	For Jack to be pain free	1 Full physical investigations carried out by GP to rule out any physical causes 2 Blood tests to be ordered and obtained 3 Pain relief to be offered during investigations	Weekly by care coordinator
2 Loss of appetite	For Jack to enjoy his food again	1 Complete physical investigations above to rule out physical cause 2 Advise and discuss diet, eating habits, etc.	Weekly by care coordinator
3 Unable to sleep	To develop regular sleep pattern	1 Jack to keep sleep diary recording length and quality of sleep 2 Discuss activities that promote/ interfere with sleep and rest	Weekly by care coordinator
4 Missing school/ education	To encourage regular attendance at school	1 Discuss with Jack any worries about schoolwork 2 Encourage Jack to develop coping skills in managing symptoms 3 Refer to psychiatrist to assess mental health needs	Weekly by care coordinator and psychiatrist/ GP

more questions before it is decided who is the most appropriate person to plan care with Jack. Therefore the example care plan in Table 5.2 is provided based upon what we know from the scenario.

Note In all mental health assessments all physical investigations must be carried out first in order to rule out physical causes and to treat symptoms effectively and quickly.

Conclusion

This chapter has drawn upon legal, ethical and theoretical frameworks in the care of children and young people who may experience mental health problems. This area of care planning can be extremely complex and skills in assessment and care planning must be developed in order to help a young person cope with their experiences as quickly as possible.

There is also a huge mental health promotion aspect to the care of young people and children whereby helping them to prevent mental illness through developing coping skills, support networks and resilience can be of more benefit than waiting until they become ill. Governments and local authorities are driving this agenda for children and young people although mental health promotion can also filter into other local services such as schools and families. Therefore personalised mental health care for children and young people must recognise the context and complexity within the mental health services in meeting the needs of young people.

References

Butts, J. and Rich, K. (2005) *Nursing Ethics: Across the Curriculum and into Practice*. London: Jones Bartlett.

Cobb, J. (2006) Interventions in child and adolescent mental health, in Chapter 2, Essential mental health nursing skills. In P. Callaghan and H. Waldock (eds) *Oxford Handbook of Mental Health Nursing*. Oxford: Oxford University Press.

Davidson, J. (chair) (2008) *Children and Young People in Mind: Final Report of the National CAMHS Review*. London: Department of Health.

DH (Department of Health) (2008) *Code of Practice Mental Health Act 1983*. London: TSO.

DH (2009) *New Horizons: A Shared Vision for Mental Health*. London: Department of Health.

DH (2011) *No Health Without Mental Health: A Cross Governmental Mental Health Outcomes Strategy for People of all Ages*. London: Department of Health.

Feat, J. (2005) Law and social policy relating to children. In M. Cooper, C. Hooper and M.Thompson (eds) *Child and Adolescent Mental Health: Theory and Practice*. London: Hodder Arnold, pp. 28–38.

Holyoake, D.D. (2005) Child and adolescent mental health services (CAMHS): taking care of business on the unit! In R. Tummey (ed.) *Planning Care in Mental Health Nursing*. Basingstoke: Palgrave MacMillan, pp. 167–84.

Jane-Lopis, E. and Anderson, P. (2007) A policy framework for the promotion of mental health and the prevention of mental disorders. In M. Knapp, D. McDaid, E. Mossialos and G. Thornicroft (eds) *Mental Health Policy and Practice Across Europe: The Future Direction of Mental Health Care*. Maidenhead: Open University Press, pp. 188–214.

Limmerick, M. (2006) Assessing children and adolescents, in Chapter 2, Essential mental health nursing skills. In P. Callaghan and H. Waldock (eds) *Oxford Handbook of Mental Health Nursing*. Oxford: Oxford University Press.

Maughan, B. (2011) Family and systemic influences. In D. Skuse, H. Bruce, L. Dowdney and D. Mrazek (eds) *Child Psychology and Psychiatry: Frameworks for Practice*, 2nd edn. Chichester: Wiley.

Pressley, M. and McCormack, C.B. (2007) *Child and Adolescent Development for Educators*. New York: Guilford Press.

RCP (2010) *Who's Who in CAMHS*. London: Royal College of Psychiatrists.

Vick, C. and Nicolas, A. (2005) Aetiology. In M. Cooper, C. Hooper and M. Thompson (eds) *Child and Adolescent Mental Health: Theory and Practice*. London: Hodder Arnold.

6 Person-centred care planning for people with learning disabilities who have mental health needs

Carl Benton, Mark Jukes and Marie O'Boyle-Duggan

Learning outcomes

After reading this chapter you will be able to

- Establish why people with a learning disability are more likely to have mental health needs.
- Identify appropriate assessments (including risk) to enable effective person centred care planning
- Differentiate between challenging behaviour and mental health in a learning disabled population
- Define the practitioner's role for this service user population

Introduction

It appears paradoxical that only as recently as the 1980s, it was generally believed by professionals that people with a learning disability did not have the cognitive capacity to actually experience mental health difficulties. Equally, this view also applied to accessing psychotherapeutic services, where from Carl Rogers' perspective in 1957, people with learning disabilities would not be able to access client centred therapy for similar reasons (Sinason 2002; Smiley 2005). However, both these perspectives have positively and significantly changed, particularly since the 1960s, through advances in our knowledge and understanding of mental health needs as experienced by people with a learning disability. Application of psychological therapies are also made more readily available to people with a learning disability (Brandon 1989; Waitman and Conboy-Hill 1992; Sinason 2002; Jukes and Aldridge 2006).

So as not to cause confusion for those reading this chapter, when a patient with a learning disability and a mental health problem is diagnosed, we use the term dual-diagnosis, as it refers to the diagnosis of a learning disability with a mental health problem. This term, however is not to be confused with the use in mental health services, where dual-diagnosis refers to a patient who misuses substances such as alcohol or drugs and which contributes to the type of mental health problem the patient experiences. However, recent research has identified that there is a small but increasing number of people with learning disabilities living independently who can, and do, develop substance misuse problems, and are sometimes targeted due to their vulnerability (Huxley et al. 2007).

The policy document *Valuing People* (DH 2001) was the first strategic government policy directive in thirty years since 1971 for people with a learning disability, where its agenda was specifically to tackle social exclusion. Its targets for both children and adults with a learning disability embrace four themes of rights, choice, inclusion and independence which should be seen to resonate throughout all relationships and services which focus around the individual.

Since Mencap's report *Death by Indifference* (2007), which led to the *Six-Lives* (2009) report by the Ombudsman, and the Michael Report (Michael 2008), *Healthcare for All*, much emphasis has been placed upon the need to support people with a learning disability with dignity and respect when being admitted into acute hospital care. Currently, the evidence base from such reports highlights a number of key variables relating specifically to general hospital staff and the service or organization that influences the access to general hospital services as indicated in Table 6.1.

The Royal College of Psychiatrists (1998) acknowledged that enabling people with learning disabilities to use ordinary mental health services is a complex and

Table 6.1 Comparison of findings in acute general and mental health care settings

General hospital settings	*Acute mental health care settings*
Hospital staff not understanding the specific health needs of people with a learning disability	Staff lack training and experience in the assessment and treatment of this client group
Problems with communication and behaviour – and a lack of knowledge of how to deal with these	Problems of targeting specific interventions and the rapid pace of life
Under-/overprotectiveness	May be exposed to influences such as smoking, alcohol, illegal drugs and sexual relationships for the first time on an acute ward
Carers having to stay with people to provide basic care	Vulnerable to all forms of exploitation (including sexual abuse)
Negative attitudes and a lack of confidence of hospital staff working with people with a learning disability	Acute wards often have very high bed occupancy and a rapid turnover of patients – could lead to 'bed blocking' by patients with a learning disability
A lack of learning disability-specific training included within pre- and post-registration training for healthcare professionals	

Source: Day (1993); Bouras and Holt (1997, 2001); Chaplin and Flynn (2000); Kwok (2001); Hannon and Clift (2011).

demanding task requiring input from specialists in the psychiatry of learning disability. Recent policy directives explicitly state that people who have both a learning disability and additional mental health needs should have access to mainstream health services. However, as well as having access to generic services, people with a learning disability should still have additional support from specialist learning disability services when this is required (Ferguson 2009).

When people with a learning disability have accessed mental health services, several factors and concerns have been highlighted in relation to admitting adults with learning disabilities into general adult mental health wards. These factors can be seen to have similar themes and experiences to those which people with a learning disability have found within acute hospital settings, with additional findings that in some cases people who have a learning disability are often vulnerable to exploitation, including sexual abuse by more intellectually able and, at times, disturbed patients.

Prevalence

In terms of assessing the prevalence rates of mental ill health in people with a learning disability, this area has been fraught with methodological limitations, which include biased sampling, reliance upon existing case-file information, or from instruments which have been designed as screening tools. Further limitations include whether these rates are based on lifetime or point prevalence, combined prevalence rates for children and adults, and including adults who only have verbal communication.

Recent research into the epidemiology of mental health needs in people with learning disabilities puts prevalence rates between 20.1 per cent and 22.41 per cent, which excludes challenging behaviour in adults (Taylor et al. 2004; Cooper et al. 2007) compared to 16 per cent in the wider population (DH 2003).

The study by Cooper et al. (2007) is based upon a large-scale population-based study with clearly described methods and where each participant ($n = 1023$) underwent a detailed assessment by skilled specialists in learning disabilities, along with a detailed face to face assessment supported by their paid or family carer. The findings identified that the most prevalent mental health disorders apart from the more general behaviour problems (22.5 per cent), included autism spectrum disorders (7.5 per cent), affective disorders (6.6 per cent) and psychotic disorders (4.4 per cent). More specific but less prevalent disorders included anxiety disorders (3.8 per cent), pica (2.0 per cent) and alcohol/substance misuse and personality disorders (1.0 per cent). It is important to discover the prevalence of the mental health needs of people with learning disabilities so that services can be developed in order to meet their needs and also for care coordinators to help the person to find information to support and plan care.

Over one in three children and adolescents with a learning disability in Britain (36 per cent) have a diagnosable psychiatric disorder compared to 10 per cent in children from the wider population (DH 2005b). Children and adolescents with learning disabilities are over six times more likely to have a diagnosable psychiatric disorder than their peers who do not have learning disabilities (Emerson and Hatton 2007). In terms of increased risk for children having a mental health problem, Emerson and Hatton (2007) further identify that the pervasiveness of mental health needs cuts across all types of psychiatric disorders. The increased risks for children of having a mental health problem are as follows:

- 33 times more likely to have an autistic spectrum condition;
- 8 times more likely to have attention deficit hyperactive disorder (ADHD);
- 6 times more likely to have a conduct disorder;
- 4 times more likely to have an emotional disorder;
- 1.7 times more likely to have a depressive disorder.

Emerson and Hatton (2007) place additional emphasis on the social context to these types of mental health needs in children, where nearly two thirds of children with emotional disorders are living in poverty and six out of ten have been exposed to two or more different types of adverse life events. Over half of children are supported by a mother who is likely to have mental health needs herself.

The whole landscape of provision of services for both people with mental health needs and people with a learning disability has markedly changed, with the emphasis on service user-led outcomes. Since the implementation of the *National Service Framework for Mental Health* (NSF) (DH 1999), *Valuing People* (DH 2001, 2009b) and *New Horizons* (2009a) emphasise that learning disability services are required to work closely with those professionals implementing the Mental Health NSF to meet the needs of people with learning disabilities and mental health needs.

Person centred planning in England has significantly influenced the field of learning disability, and is echoed within such policy strategy documents as *Valuing People* (DH 2001, 2009b) and has much to offer the field of mental health in its approaches to person centred thinking and tools for assessment and practice.

Person centred planning is the capability in seeing people first rather than relating to diagnostic labels; using ordinary language and images rather than professional jargon; actively searching for a person's gifts and capacities in the context of community life; and strengthening the voice of the person and those who know the person best in accounting for their history, evaluating their present conditions in terms of valued experiences, and defining desirable changes in their lives (Mount 1992). When a person with a learning disability and mental health difficulties is admitted as a patient into a specialist service for assessment and treatment, it is essential that practitioners in mental health and learning disability begin to challenge the 'old' or traditional conceptual framework for assessment and planning, and develop a new 'person focused' conceptual framework for practice and engagement as interpreted in Table 6.2.

Table 6.2 Person focused conceptual framework for practice and engagement

The 'old' conceptual framework for assessment and planning	A new conceptual framework
Start with what is wrong with the person	Start with how the person wants to live
	Learn what is important to the person in everyday life
Assess issues of health and safety	Assess issues of health and safety
Determine what the person can and cannot do	Assess what the person might want to learn to get more of what is important
Assessments of adaptive behaviour	Plan with the person
Strengths and needs list	Describe what is important to the person
Plans that describe how to keep the person healthy and safe and that 'make' them more independent	Describe what others need to know or do to support the person
	Address any issues of health or safety in the context of how the person wants to live
	Offer opportunities for learning that help the person get more of what the person wants
	As the person gets more of what is important in everyday life look for opportunities for the person to spend time in places and doing things where they are welcomed by the others there
	As the person spends time where they are welcomed, look for opportunities to help establish and nurture relationships
	Seek to discover what the person might like in the future and help them move in that direction

Source: Smull (2000).

The Care Programme Approach

The Care Programme Approach (CPA) (DH 1990) was introduced to provide a coordinated and multiprofessional collaborative framework across health boundaries for those with mental health needs leaving hospital or living in the community. Its focus was to ensure each service user had an assessment of need and risk, a comprehensive care plan, a relapse/crisis plan and an allocated care co-ordinator within a robust review system. It aimed to ensure service users received appropriate levels of support to maintain them in the community and reduce the risk of admission to hospital for those that may harm themselves or others. Following public and government concern over a number of homicides and suicides a review of such cases indicated a number of similarities (Eastman 1996; see Table 6.3). It is important to recognise factors that will impact on delivering quality care and how using CPA can positively enhance care planning and outcome measures.

Table 6.3 Report of the Confidential Inquiry into Homicides and Suicides by Mentally Ill People

Key problems	Key recommendations
Failures of communication between professionals	Strengthening risk assessment skills in clinical teams
Lack of clarity about care plans	Increasing face to face contact time with patients
Lack of time for face to face contact with patients	Supporting the development of genuine multi-disciplinary teams
Need for additional staff training	Developing better systems for communication between professionals and between professionals and families
Poor compliance with treatment by patients	
Insufficient use of legal powers to supervise patients at risk	Raising awareness about appropriate uses of legal powers under the Mental Health Act 1983 through further training
	Ensuring that treatment environments are acceptable for patients

Source: Eastman (1996).

Activity 6.1   Critical reflection: Care Programme Approach

1 Reflect on your experiences so far and think about the skills required to be a care coordinator and how the role of care coordination is allocated.
2 Does the CPA in your area reflect the principles of person centred planning and how are they applied?

The Psychiatric Assessment Schedule for Adults with Developmental Disabilities (PAS-ADD)

The assessment of mental health issues in people with a learning disability is, in many ways, similar to those within mainstream mental health services. However a number of factors need to be considered, such as communication, cognitive ability, environmental factors and behavioural phenotypes. Utilizing a standardised, evidenced based assessment tool can support clinical opinions and lead to an enhanced assessment. One such tool is the Psychiatric Assessment Schedule for Adults with Developmental Disabilities (PAS-ADD; Moss 2002), which has been developed since the early 1990s (Moss et al. 1993). Although other tools are available (PIMRA, Matson et al. 1984; REISS, Reiss 1988) the authors' suggest that the PAS-ADD (Moss 2002) is more consistently applied by learning disability professionals and services, and this assertion is shared by Devine and Taggart (2008),

Table 6.4 PAS-ADD checklist and case study examples

	In the last four weeks			
Question	Has not happened or has always been like this	Happened occasionally or present in a mild form	Happened frequently or present in a moderate form	Present in a severe form for much of the time
Broken sleep, waking up for an hour or more, before falling back to sleep	0	0	1	1
Suspicious, untrusting, behaving as if someone is trying to harm them or is talking about them	0	0	1	1
Avoids social contact more than usual for the person	0	0	1	1

The PAS-ADD (Moss 2002) has three schedules: a PAS-ADD checklist, a mini PAS-ADD and PAS-ADD clinical interview (originally the PAS-ADD 10). The PAS-ADD checklist is a screening tool looking at significant life events (previous two years) and 25 factors across affective, psychosis and organic disorders during the previous four week period, which enables clinicians to decide if further assessments are indicated (examples from the checklist are given in Table 6.4). Each of these schedules will add depth to assessment, treatment and reviews. There are training and supervision needs for staff utilizing this system which need to be addressed by clinicians to adhere to governance frameworks.

Case study – Paul

Paul is a 22-year-old man who has been diagnosed with a mild learning disability and an autistic spectrum condition and who has been referred to the mental health centre you currently work within by his GP. Paul has recently lost his part time job at a local factory after displaying bizarre behaviour, including hitting and kicking another member of staff. The victim reported it to the police and Paul was interviewed by the police but no charges were brought. Currently Paul lives with his elderly grandparents following the death of his mother 18 months ago. His mother and father split up when Paul was 12, his father moved away from the area and has little contact with him. Paul has no siblings. Over the last eight weeks Paul has been telling his grandparents that people have been watching him at work and that a local group of youths has been following him. Paul seems to have difficulty concentrating, appears confused at times and has also recently stopped watching television as he thinks the people on the television are trying to talk to him and put thoughts into his head. The grandparents have noticed that he has stopped looking after himself, rarely washes or showers, and has developed a poor sleep pattern. Although Paul used to like being in the lounge with his grandparents he is staying in his bedroom and does not like to leave the house on his own. Since leaving school Paul has lost contact with his friends and does not socialise apart from his grandparents' friends.

Out of 18 life events highlighted Paul would tick the following boxes:

- death of a first degree relative;
- move of house or residence;
- laid off or sacked from work;
- problems with police or other authority.

Activity 6.2   Critical reflection: ensuring person centred approaches

Think about the following:

1   What factors do you need to consider in your initial assessment of Paul?
2   Who would you like to interview, giving your rationale, and how would you go about this?
3   Which other professionals would you involve and why?
4   Using the CPA care plan what would you include?
5   Should Paul access mainstream mental health services or specialist learning disability services? What would be your rationale for the decision?

Once you have given these questions some thought look at the sample CPA care plan in Table 6.6. It is important to build an effective therapeutic relationship with Paul and discover his thoughts about his condition and his future aspirations. In the first instance risk assessment and management is important to ensure people's safety, including Paul's. This can be achieved via the CPA risk documentation, or by developing a safety action plan or risk reduction plan (Aldridge 2007). An example of a Care Plan and Early Warning Signs monitoring sheet can be seen in Table 6.4 above.

Table 6.5 A ten-step person-centred risk assessment

Ten steps to safety planning

Part A	Person-centred risk assessment
Step 1	Describe the risk and identify the level of risk
Step 2	Involve and inform all the stakeholders throughout the process
Step 3	Describe the setting conditions or context of the risk
Step 4	Describe the triggers or antagonizing factors
Step 5	Describe the helpful or protagonizing factors
Step 6	Identify the advantages and disadvantages of taking the risk
Part B	Developing a person-centred safety plan
Step 7	Identify the aim of the safety plan
Step 8	Explore the options for reducing the level of risk
Step 9	Decide on the least restrictive, effective alternative from your list
Step 10	Write the safety action plan or a full risk reduction plan

Source: Adapted from Aldridge (2007).

Activity 6.3 Critical reflection on structured tools

From your own experiences, what mental health assessments are used in your practice area? Think about how a structured tool like the PAS-ADD (Moss 2002) could enhance your understanding of a person with a mental health need and a learning disability.

Aldridge (2007) developed a ten-step person centred risk assessment and safety plan (see Table 6.5). When completing such a risk assessment with the service user, it is essential to enable and develop a therapeutic relationship, while building trust and respect. It also gives the service user an opportunity to develop some ownership and insight, and for them to offer some meaningful coping/management strategies. The reader may be aware and have experienced other forms of risk assessment strategies and models, which could be applied to formulate a risk management plan.

Activity 6.4 Critical reflection on risk assessment

Think about risk assessment tools you have encountered and how useful they were to the service user and the multiprofessional group.

Conceptual frameworks

Conceptual models are important when considering assessment and treatment pathways in order for teams and individuals to make sense of their values and beliefs about service users and clinical practice. The landscape of learning disability nursing has changed significantly since the early 2000s, and continues to evolve where learning disability nurses are demonstrating and applying conceptual frameworks as part of their practice.

In Table 6.6, four conceptual models are highlighted that could provide practitioners with a way of delivering care from a person centred planning paradigm (Sweeney and Sanderson 2002). Each model embeds person centred approaches and places the service user at the centre of their care. The importance of the therapeutic relationship (Peplau 1952) is emphasised and our ability to effectively communicate enhances the quality of the interaction.

Activity 6.5   Critical reflection on conceptual frameworks

1   What conceptual frameworks have you experienced and do you consider them to have values and concepts which embrace a person-centred ethos?
2   What factors would influence the introduction of the use of a nursing model in your current service area?
3   What specific features would influence your personal preference of one nursing model over another?

Diagnostic overshadowing

Activity 6.6   Guided imagery

Imagine a situation where you feel physically unwell, have headaches, aches and pains. Your course of action might be to remain in bed and rest, maybe take some form of analgesia. You might need to telephone someone to say you will not be attending a place of work or study.

If you were an individual with severe learning disabilities those around you might not understand what you are trying to communicate. Therefore how would you tell someone else how unwell you are feeling and how will they know?

You have decided to stay in bed and rest or it could be that you are too ill to get up and yet your carer is demanding that you get up because you have to

Table 6.6 Conceptual frameworks

Key philosophy	Core concepts	Intervention focus
Tidal model – Phil Barker and Poppy Buchanan-Barker (2005)		
Collaborative approach reflective of personalization theory It emphasises that people are unique and the pathway is from the lowest ebb to everyday community life. Focuses on supporting people when they are most distressed and begins the process of self-management at earliest opportunity	There are three personal domains: self, world and others which provide a theoretical framework for the following processes Change is inevitable, nothing lasts whether joy or pain The person's experience is unique and we can never fully understand another person's experience, positive or negative Enable the person to reclaim their story	Holistic assessment, one-to-one sessions, personal security plan and the three forms of group work – discovery, solutions and information-sharing
Peplau model (1952)		
A shared experience between the service user and the nurse	A psychodynamic model which emphasises the importance of the interpersonal and therapeutic relationship The nurse has seven dynamic roles: stranger, resource, teacher, counsellor, surrogate, leader and technical expert	The relationship has a pathway of four phases: orientation, identification, exploitation and resolution
Neuman's model (1995)		
Holistic interdisciplinary approach	Views individuals as open systems that interact with internal and external environments to maintain a balance between three types of stressors (intrapersonal, interpersonal and extrapersonal) which can be positive or negative depending on the person's ability to cope at any given time	Five major stages 1 initial nursing diagnosis 2 stressors perceived by service user 3 stressors perceived by caregiver 4 personal factors 5 comprehensive nursing diagnosis
Aldridge and Ferguson ecology of mental health framework (2007)		
Multiprofessional approach to develop a hypothesis as a way of understanding the dynamics of mental health within a learning disability perspective	People's behaviour influenced by the interrelationship between a large number of factors These various factors may impact on an individual's mental health	Triangulated approach to assessment to understand causal and maintenance factors Domains – personal, environmental, interpersonal

go out today to work/day care. What often happens for a person with learning difficulties at this point is to be described as challenging by their carer, because as they see it you are refusing to participate in daily living activities.

Take this scenario further and consider what it might be like if the individual has suffered a recent loss, is feeling sad and low in mood, but cannot verbalise or understand these feelings. At which point in this scenario might you become angry or upset if it was you, would you hit out at a carer or swear and shout or become upset and withdrawn?

Challenging behaviour

The following is a working definition of challenging behaviour used within many learning disability services, first termed by Emerson (1997: 4) as 'Culturally abnormal behaviours of such an intensity, frequency or duration that the physical safety of the person or others is likely to be placed in serious jeopardy, or behaviour which is likely to seriously limit or deny access to and use of ordinary community facilities'. Therefore when an individual with learning disabilities displays behavioural change, this is often attributed to their learning disability, rather than a psychiatric disorder. Consequently the individual's physical or emotional/psychological distress or illness is misdiagnosed and thought to be due to the learning disability resulting in the term 'diagnostic overshadowing' (Stanton and Coetzee 2004; Mason and Scior 2004). Reiss et al. (1982) suggest people with Down's syndrome are susceptible to dementia, which could be missed because of diagnostic overshadowing.

Activity 6.7   Critical reflection on challenging behaviour

Think about a service user with learning disabilities that you have worked with who has displayed challenging behaviour or any behavioural change.

List these behaviours and then categorise them into two columns, one headed mental health, and the second as learning disabilities.

Having completed your list consider the following questions:

- Which behaviours did you attribute to mental health and which to learning disabilities?
- Did you have any overlap of behaviours?
- What have you learned from this exercise about how you perceive behaviours?
- Were issues of diagnostic overshadowing present?

Psychosocial masking

Sovner (1986) highlighted four factors reflecting the effects of learning disability that may influence the diagnostic process:

- **Intellectual distortion** – emotional symptoms may be difficult to obtain because of deficits in abstract thinking and in receptive and expressive language skills in some individuals with learning disabilities.
- **Psychosocial masking** – limited life experiences can influence the content of psychiatric symptoms; symptoms may have a less complex presentation which may lead to severe symptoms being missed.
- **Cognitive disintegration** – a decreased ability to tolerate stress can lead to anxiety-induced decompensation sometimes misinterpreted as psychosis. Cognitive disintegration refers to a disruption in cognitive or mental functioning such as attention, memory, and goal-directed behaviour. Decompensation means that anxiety, stress, depression or other mental conditions cause a person for a period of time to lose their ability to perform normal activities of daily living, such as relationships with other people, or to maintain normal concentration, persistence, or pace.
- **Baseline exaggeration** – the severity or frequency of pre-existing chronic maladaptive behaviour or cognitive deficits may increase after onset of psychiatric illness.

The following are some indicators of how mental health may be presented in people with a learning disability (adapted from Hardy and Bouras 2002).

For reflection purposes, are some of the behavioural changes highlighted below on your own list identified as a challenging behaviour or mental health need?

- changes in sleep pattern, appetite and weight;
- reduction in overall self-help skills, reduced concentration;
- changes in behaviour, increase in challenging behaviour;
- communication levels, conflict in relationships;
- withdrawal from social contact and activity or disinhibition;
- increase or decrease in activity levels;
- irritability, memory difficulties;
- difficulties adapting to changes in environment or situations;
- changes in perception of themselves and those around them.

Challenging behaviour should be seen in the context of where the individual lives, works or who they interact with. As practitioners we need to undertake a person centred holistic assessment, where challenging behaviour may be caused and identified by a number of factors (RCN 2010):

- mental illness
- learned behaviour
- trauma
- pain

- physical illness
- neurobiological factors
- communication needs
- environmental issues
- abuse
- behavioural phenotypes.

It is frequently found that staff working with individuals with learning disabilities avoid and misunderstand those clients who challenge (Hastings 2002; Hastings and Brown 2002). However, increased staff engagement in client interactions, as a result of proactive approaches to challenging behaviour such as 'positive behaviour support' (Jones et al. 2001; Eber et al. 2002; Mansell et al. 2002), as well as sound evidence based interventions within an 'applied behaviour analysis' model (Heineman and Dunlap 2000; Whitaker 2002) is apparent.

Positive behavioural support (PBS) consists of the conceptual framework of applied behaviour analysis combined with the value based approaches of social role valorization (Wolfensberger 1983) and person centred planning and care (Osgood 2009). What positive behaviour support aims to do is reduce restrictive and aversive practice and promote positive support for people whose behaviour services find challenging. Legally and ethically public sector services and practitioners have a legal duty to provide reasonable adjustments (DH 1995), which include: removing barriers that exist in terms of access to services, service delivery and ensuring that policies, procedures and staff training all enable services to work equally well for people with learning disabilities (Hatton et al. 2010) and to support individuals to make decisions through an articulation and application of the Mental Capacity Act (DH 2005a). The mental health needs of people with profound and multiple learning disabilities have been greatly neglected in terms of services, knowledge and understanding according to Sheehy and Nind (2005), who identify four inter-relating factors:

- becoming a person, having thoughts and feelings;
- deficit based services giving a deficient service;
- being excluded through lack of voice;
- communication barriers.

They further suggest that people with profound and multiple learning disabilities are more vulnerable to mental ill health than other individuals with learning disabilities and the wider population, and strongly recommend that the way forward is to achieve a better understanding of the emotional wellbeing of people with mental health and learning disabilities.

Role of the practitioner

As mental health practitioners it is important that you are inclusive in your practice and systematic in your approach; consideration should be given to how and where an individual's mental health needs should be met. Assessment is the most important part of care planning and delivery (DH 2000; Sox 2004), especially when referred due to challenging behaviour. A physical health screening assessment, 'OK' Health Check (Matthews 2004), identifies physiological illness and conditions common in people with learning disabilities, including mental health needs. Diagnosis is crucial because this determines a person's eligibility to access an appropriate service to meet needs.

As part of any assessment practitioners need to be aware of suggestibility and acquiescence, as suggested by Clare and Gudjonsson (1993), which is reported to be common in learning disabilities.

Suggestibility can occur with leading questions, therefore more thought needs to be given to how questions are phrased, or they could potentially lead the person to answer with what they think the interviewer wants to hear. To acquiesce is when the individual covers up limitations in an attempt to hide their disability, adopting a cloak of competence (Edgerton 1993). Therefore it is important to consider how these difficulties may be pursued through a person centred relationship.

Activity 6.8   Critical reflective point

How might you approach any of the conditions highlighted above, when assisting in assessing and providing care for the mental health needs of a person with learning disabilities?

Consider the guided imagery activity earlier – feeling low in mood, suffering loss symptoms. From a person centred perspective, what would your assumptions and expectations be through the development of a professional and patient centred relationship?

As discussed earlier, confusion can occur in assessment and diagnosis of individuals with learning disabilities and presenting mental health problems. Table 6.7 highlights possible normal and abnormal behaviours as a comparison to aid assessment.

Interventions

Intervention should be person centred and holistic with consideration given to the inclusion of proactive and reactive strategies. This may include changing the environment, teaching new skills, providing appropriate activities, direct treatment and consideration of ways to ensure provision of positive behavioural support to the individual.

Table 6.7 Normal and abnormal behaviour characteristics

Possible normal behaviour in someone with learning disabilities	Abnormal behaviour in the context of mental health problems
Echoing – repeating what they have heard. Very common in people with autism Overactive – may be very active but not meet the threshold for any psychiatric diagnosis. The overactivity is part of the person's personality and has a consistent pattern Very active imagination or fantasy world, such as having imaginary friends	Echolalia – may be helpful in diagnosing major psychoses such as schizophrenia. Can also be present in autistic spectrum disorders Hypomanic – behaves differently from how they would normally. As well as being overactive, thought processes may also be abnormal (e.g. feeling grandiose and have racing thoughts). May become disinhibited or promiscuous Auditory hallucinations and delusions, indicative of a psychiatric illness

Source: Adapted from RCN (2010).

A constructional approach was first described by Goldiamond (1974), based within learning theory and developed in applied behaviour analysis. When applied to clinical intervention the focus is on the construction of new skills, reinstatement of skills demonstrated in the past, and the transfer of current skills to new situations. Table 6.8 shows the authors' adapted use of a constructional framework applied to a person centred, holistic nursing approach.

Mental health practitioners have a valid and essential role in the care of people with learning disabilities. It is therefore important that the necessary resources are available to provide quality assessments and treatment/intervention, which effectively means collaboration within and across services, and with a variety of professionals across health, social care and the independent sector and which includes learning disability practitioners.

The following list highlights the role practitioners can apply in meeting the mental health needs of people with a learning disabillity:

- Awareness of vulnerability factors
- Increasing protective factors
- Health promotion to service users, their families and carers
- Awareness of mental health presentation in people with learning disabilities
- Awareness of screening tools available
- Referral to appropriate services and support
- Systematic assessment and positive behavioural support/interventions

Table 6.8 An adapted constructional framework for mental health interventions for individuals with learning disabilities

	Proactive strategies 'Protective factors'		Reactive strategies
Environment	Positive programming Positive behavioural support	Direct treatment	Risk assessment
Stable environment	Development of social skills	Adequate nutrition and exercise	Risk management
Supportive skilled staff	General skills	Detection and treatment of physical illness	Active listening
Being listened to and involved in planning care	Developmental skills Communication	Positive behavioural strategies	Stimulus control Non-touch distraction
Access to support services	Alternative behaviours	Positive behavioural strategies	Crisis response
Occupation	Coping and tolerance	Differential schedules of reinforcement	
Ethnic and cultural needs met	Social skills (assertiveness, dealing with conflict)	Cognitive behaviour therapy	
Economic security	Anxiety management	Medication	
Being part of community/ peer group	Intensive interaction		
Non-aversive approaches/ responses			

Source: Adapted from Hardy and Bouras (2002).

- Accessible interventions and information applicable to the individual's level of understanding
- Preparation of individual for in-patient or transition through services.

The care plan for Paul in Table 6.9 provides an overview of Paul's needs and how these might be addressed. While it is presented and written in a slightly different way to other care plans in this book, the main features of the APIE model can be identified within the columns and evaluation will take place separately on another sheet.

It is also important when planning care for a person who has learning disabilities that they can become involved in planning their care and that they can understand their care plan. Using pictures and mood charts that show faces with a range of emotions may help people with learning disabilities become more involved in their care plan and provide evidence that their plan of care becomes personalised to their own individual needs. Similarly it is important to use language that everyone can understand and avoid using professional jargon that can exclude rather than include the person. Using the person's own words as shown in the care plan in Table 6.9 can help to avoid confusion and ensure that the care plan is effective in meeting Paul's personalised needs.

Table 6.9 Care plan for Paul

Assessment	Planning	Implementation	Evaluation
1 I need help to assess my mental health	I will have completed an assessment	I will see a psychiatrist and a nurse who will assess me	Monthly
2 My grandparents need help to support me	My grandparents will be assessed	A social worker will do a carer's assessment for my grandparents	Monthly
3 How do I keep myself safe	I will have completed a risk assessment and relapse plan	The people involved will do a risk assessment and look at things that may be harmful to me or other people	Monthly
4 I would like another job	I will have some daytime activity	When I am feeling better the nurse and occupational therapist will help me look for a job	3 Monthly
5 I would like to meet some friends	I will be able to take part in activities with others	The nurse and social worker will see if they can look for some social groups or activities	Monthly
6 I would like to visit my dad	I will be able to visit my dad	The social worker will talk to my dad	Monthly

Conclusion

This chapter has attempted to grapple with major challenges when engaging with people with learning disabilities who have additional mental health needs. Such challenges range from service-user access and inclusion perspectives, through to clinical assessment and interventional strategies adopted by a range of healthcare professionals and which includes nurses in mental health and learning disability. Recent health policy has identified gross inadequacies in both mainstream and mental health provision for people with learning disabilities in an era when contemporary ideology gravitates away from traditional paternalistic and professionally orientated health and social care provision. Mental health and learning disability practitioners are required to identify with the person so that together they can work towards resolutions which resonate with their personal vision for a quality and person centred way of living, embracing the individual's mental health needs.

Assessment and interventions depend on our ability to accurately interpret the person's world experience using appropriate communication systems to understand the effects of the environment. Additionally, the person's world views and direct experiences of the healthcare system influence the way in which people with learning disabilities with additional mental health needs can survive, not only in personalised services, but also when admitted for assessment and treatment within specialised services.

Practitioners are required to assess the degree of mental health need and to be skilled and discriminatory in separating out ambiguous signs and symptoms. Such signs and symptoms, to the unskilled eye, may put down behaviours as part of the person's learning disability or suggestive of a challenging behaviour. People with a learning disability have more susceptibility to developing a mental health need so it is critical that practitioners in mental health services are equipped to support the person with additional knowledge and competency.

References

Aldridge, J. (2007) Fundamental nursing concepts: risk assessment, risk management and safety planning. In M. Jukes and J. Aldridge (eds) *Person-centred Practices: A Holistic and Integrated Approach*. London: Quay Books.

Aldridge, J. and Fergusson, D. (2007) Models for practice: the ecology of mental health framework. In M. Jukes and J. Aldridge (eds) *Person-centred Practices: A Holistic and Integrated Approach*. London: Quay Books.

Barker, P. and Buchanan-Barker, P. (2005) *The Tidal Model: A Guide for Mental Health Professionals*. London and New York: Brunner-Routledge.

Bouras, N. and Holt, G. (1997) Crisis in London's mental health services, meeting the needs of people with learning disabilities would unblock acute beds (Letter). *British Medical Journal*, 314: 1278–9.

Bouras, N. and Holt, G. (2001) Community mental health services for adults with learning disabilities. In G. Thornicroft and G. Szmukler (eds) *Textbook of Common Psychiatry*. Oxford: Oxford University Press, pp. 397–407.

Brandon, D. (ed.) (1989) *Mutual Respect: Therapeutic Approaches to Working with People who have Learning Difficulties*. Surbiton: Good Impressions.

Chaplin, R. and Flynn, A. (2000) Adults with learning disability admitted to psychiatric wards. *Advances in Psychiatric Treatment*, 6: 128–34.

Clare, I.C. and Gudjonsson, G.H. (1993) Interrogative suggestibility, confabulation and acquiescence in people with mild learning disabilities (mental handicap): implications for reliability during police interrogations. *British Journal of Clinical Psychology*, 32(3): 295–301.

Cooper, S-A., Smiley, E., Morrison, J., Williamson, A. and Allan, L. (2007) Mental ill-health in adults with intellectual disabilities: prevalence and associated factors. *British Journal of Psychiatry*, 190: 27–35.

Day, K.A. (1993) Mental health services for people with mental retardation: a framework for the future. *Journal of Intellectual Disability Research*, 37: 7–16.

DH (Department of Health) (1990) *The Care Programme Approach for People with a Mental Illness Referred to Specialist Psychiatric Services*. HC(90)23/LASSL(90)11. London: Joint Health and Social Services Circular, Department of Health.

DH (1995) *Disability Discrimination Act*. London: HMSO.

DH (1999) *National Service Framework for Mental Health: Modern Standards and Service Models*. London: TSO.

DH (2000) *The NHS Plan: A Plan for Investment, A Plan for Reform*. London: The Stationery Office.

DH (2001) *Valuing People: A New Strategy for People with Learning Disabilities in the 21st Century*. London: The Stationery Office.

DH (2003) *Better or Worse: A Longitudinal Study of the Mental Health of Adults living in Private Households in Great Britain*. London: DH.

DH (2005a) *Mental Capacity Act*. London: HMSO.

DH (2005b) *Mental Health of Children and Young People in Great Britain*. London: The Stationery Office.

DH (2009a) *New Horizons: A Shared Vision for Mental Health*. London: The Stationery Office.

DH (2009b) *Valuing People Now*. London: The Stationery Office.

Devine, M. and Taggart, L. (2008) Addressing the mental health needs of people with learning disabilities. *Nursing Standard*, 22(45): 40–8.

Eastman, N. (1996) Inquiry into homicides by psychiatric patients: systematic audit should replace mandatory inquiries. *British Medical Journal*, 313: 1069.

Eber, L., Sugai, G., Smith, C.R. and Scott, T.M. (2002) Wraparound and positive behavioural interventions and supports in the schools. *Journal of Emotional and Behavioural Disorders*, 10(3): 171–80.

Edgerton, R.B. (1993) *The Cloak of Competence*. Berkeley and Los Angeles: University of California Press.

Emerson, E. (1997) *Challenging Behaviour: Analysis and Intervention in People with Learning Disabilities*, 2nd edn. Cambridge: Cambridge University Press.

Emerson, E. and Hatton, C. (2007) *The Mental Health of Children and Adolescents with Learning Disabilities in Britain*. Lancaster: Institute for Health Research, Lancaster University.

Ferguson, D. (2009) Mental health and learning disability. In M. Jukes (ed.) *Learning Disability Nursing Practice*. London: Quay Books, pp. 309–26.

Goldiamond, I. (1974) Toward a constructional approach to social problems: ethical and constitutional issues raised by applied behaviour analysis. *Behaviourism*, 2: 1–84.

Hannon, L. and Clift, J. (2011) *General Hospital Care for People with Learning Disabilities*. Oxford: Wiley-Blackwell.

Hardy, S. and Bouras, N. (2002) The presentation and assessment of mental health problems in people with learning disabilities. *Learning Disability Practice*, 5(3): 33–8.

Hastings, R.P. (2002) Do challenging behaviours affect staff psychological well-being? Issues of causality and mechanism. *American Journal of Mental Retardation*, 107(6): 455–67.

Hastings, R.P. and Brown, T. (2002) Coping strategies and the impact of challenging behaviours on special educators' burnout. *Mental Retardation*, 40(2): 148–56.

Hatton, C., Roberts, H. and Baines, S. (2010) *Reasonable Adjustments for People with Learning Disabilities in England: A National Survey of NHS Trusts*. Stockton on Tees: Improving Health and Lives: Learning Disabilities Observatory.

Heineman, M. and Dunlap, G. (2000) Factors affecting the outcomes of community-based behavioural support:1. Identification and description of factor categories. *Journal of Positive Behaviour Interventions*, 2: 161–9.

Huxley, A., Taggart, C., Baker, G., Castillo, L. and Barnes, D. (2007) Substance misuse amongst people with learning disabilities. *Learning Disability Today*, 7(3): 34–8.

Jones, E., Felce, D. and Lowe, K. et al. (2001) Evaluation of the dissemination of active support training in staffed community residences. *American Journal of Mental Retardation*, 106(4): 344–58.

Jukes, M. and Aldridge, J. (eds) (2006) *Person-centred Practices: A Therapeutic Perspective*. London: Quay Books.

Kwok, H.W.M. (2001) Development of a specialised psychiatric service for people with learning disabilities and mental health problems: report of a project from Kwai Chung Hospital, Hong Kong. *British Journal of Learning Disabilities*, 29: 22–5.

Mansell, J., Elliot, T., Beadle-Brown, J., Ashman, B. and Macdonald, S. (2002) Engagement in meaningful activity and 'active support' of people with intellectual disabilities in residential care. *Research in Developmental Disabilities*, 23(5): 342–52.

Mason, J. and Scior, K. (2004) Diagnostic overshadowing among clinicians working with people with intellectual disabilities in the UK. *Journal of Applied Research in Intellectual Disabilities*, 17: 85–90.

Matson, J.L., Kazdin, A.E. and Senatore, V. (1984) Psychometric properties of the psychopathology instrument for mentally retarded adults. *Applied Research in Mental Retardation*, 5: 81–90.

Matthews, D.R. (2004) *The 'OK' Health Check: Health Facilitation and Health Action Planning*, 3rd edn. Preston: Fairfield Publications.

Mencap (2007) *Death By Indifference*. London: Mencap.

Michael, J. (2008) *Healthcare For All: Report of the Independent Inquiry into Access to Healthcare for People with Learning Disabilities*. London: Department of Health.

Moss, S. (2002) *The Mini PAS-ADD Interview Pack*. Brighton: Pavilion.

Moss, S.C., Patel, P. and Prosser, H. et al. (1993) Psychiatric morbidity in older people with moderate and severe learning disability (mental retardation). Part 1: Development and reliability of the patient interview (The PAS-ADD). *British Journal of Psychiatry*, 163: 471–80.

Mount, B. (1992) *Person-centred Planning: A Sourcebook of Values, Ideas and Methods to Encourage Person-centred Development*. New York: Graphic Futures.

Osgood, T. (2009) Challenging behaviour: the contribution of nurse specialists. In M. Jukes (ed.) *Learning Disability Nursing Practice*. London: Quay Books, pp. 327–60.

Peplau, H. (1952) *Interpersonal Relationships in Nursing*. New York: G.P. Putnam & Sons.

Reiss, S. (1988) *Reiss Screen for Maladaptive Behaviour: Test Manual*, 2nd edn. Orland Park, IL: International Diagnostic Systems.

Reiss, S., Levitan, G.W. and Szyszko, J. (1982) Emotional disturbance and mental retardation: diagnostic overshadowing. *American Journal of Mental Deficiency*, 6: 567–74.

Royal College of Nursing (2010) *Mental Health Nursing of Adults with Learning Disabilities*. London: RCN.

Royal College of Psychiatrists (1998) *Psychiatric Services for Children and Adolescents with Learning Disabilities. Council Report CR70*. London: Royal College of Psychiatrists.

Sheehy, K. and Nind, N. (2005) Emotional well-being for all: mental health and people with profound and multiple learning disabilities. *British Journal of Learning Disabilities*, 33: 34–8.

Silka, V.R. and Hauser, M.J. (1997) Psychiatric assessment of the person with mental retardation. *Psychiatric Annals*, 27: 3.

Sinason, V. (2002) Treating people with learning disabilities after physical or sexual abuse. *Advances in Psychiatric Treatment*, 8: 424–32.

Smiley, E. (2005) Epidemiology of mental health problems in adults with learning disability: an update. *Advances in Psychiatric Treatment*, 11: 214–22.

Smull, M.W. and Allan, B. (2000) *Essential Lifestyle Planning and Person centred Thinking*. www.nwtdt.com/Archive/pcp/1dayoverview.pdf (accessed 9 February 2012).

Sovner, R. (1986) Limiting factors in the use of DSM–III criteria with mentally ill/mentally retarded persons. *Psychopharmacology Bulletin*, 22: 1055–9.

Sox, H.F. (2004) *Care Plans. Comprehensive Care Planning for Long Term Care Facilities: A Guide to Resident Assessment Protocols (RAPs) and Interdisciplinary Care Plans 1*. Ohio: Robin Technologies Inc.

Stanton, L.R. and Coetzee, R.H. (2004) Down's syndrome and dementia, *Advances in Psychiatric Treatment*, 10: 50–8.

Sweeney, C. and Sanderson, H. (2002) *Person-Centred Planning: BILD Factsheet No. 007*. Kidderminster: British Institute of Learning Disabilities.

Taylor, J.L., Hatton, C. and Dixon, L. et al. (2004) Screening for psychiatric symptoms: PAS-ADD checklist norms for adults with intellectual disabilities. *Journal of Intellectual Disability Research*, 48: 37–41.

Waitman, A. and Conboy-Hill, S. (1992) *Psychotherapy and Mental Handicap*. London: Sage.

Whitaker, S. (2002) Maintaining reductions in challenging behaviours: a review of the literature. *British Journal of Developmental Disabilities*, 48(Part 1, No. 94): 15–25.

Wolfensberger, W. (1983) Social role valorisation: a proposed new term for the principle of normalisation. *Mental Retardation*, 21(6): 234–9.

Useful websites

The Tidal Model http://www.tidal-model.com/

7 Mental health and older people

Rowenna Spencer, Matt Phillips and Brynley Williams

Learning outcomes

After reading this chapter you will be able to:

- Differentiate between dementia, delirium and depression in older people
- Demonstrate awareness of the basic needs of the older person with mental health problems
- Evaluate current policy and practice in the care for older people with mental health problems
- Write a personalised care plan for a person in your care

Introduction

Mental health in older people is complex due to a myriad of confounding variables including physical health issues, generational view points and stigma. The Department of Health (2001) suggest that to meet these complex needs services should promote good mental health in older people, early detection, and an integrated approach to assessment and care planning. This chapter aims to assist in giving a basis for developing an individualised care plan for the most common problems with mental health in older age and also gives you the opportunity to explore other issues to take into consideration when developing a care plan for an older person with mental health problems.

The Office of National Statistics (2009) states that in 2008 there were 18.3 million people in the UK aged 60 or older. The number of people in the UK aged 75 and over is projected to increase from 4.8 million to 8.7 million by 2033. With projected figures like this the management and efficient delivery of care for those in this category with mental health problems is going to be paramount to promoting overall health and wellbeing for an ageing nation. This chapter will discuss three main areas of practice that may be observed as depression, dementia and delirium and will provide care plans to address some of the needs that might arise.

Depression

Depression is the most common mental health problem in later life. One in four older people in the community have symptoms of depression (Craig and Mindell 2007). Depression can be a chronic disorder with many older clients having a recurrence within three years. Untreated it shortens life and increases healthcare costs as well as adding to disability from medical illnesses. However, if treated, quality of life can improve. Depression may be triggered by a variety of factors including life changes. In older people this is often because of increasing illness, frailty and loss. Loss is painful, whether it is a loss of independence, mobility, health, long term career or a relationship. Grieving over these losses is normal even if the feelings of sadness last for weeks or months. Losing all hope and joy, however, is not normal and can be attributed to depression. Depression is a disorder of mood and can be characterised by many signs and symptoms including low mood, feelings of sadness and loss of enjoyment. Some less well known characteristics associated with depression include poor memory and concentration, unexplained pain and delusional ideas.

Activity 7.1   Critical refection

Although depression in older people is a common problem only a small percentage get the help they need. Why do you think this is?

Many people believe older adults have good reason to be down or that depression is just a part of ageing. What would perhaps contribute to making people think this?

Many health professionals are likely to ignore depression in older clients. What do you think the health professionals would concentrate on instead of identifying depression?

Assessment of depression

Early recognition and prompt treatment of depression can reduce distress and sometimes prevent more serious consequences such as deteriorating physical health, personal neglect, adverse effects on relationships or self-harm and suicide. However it can often be difficult to identify depression in older people for several reasons. One such reason is that older people can present with non-specific symptoms such as tiredness or insomnia rather than disclosing depressive symptoms. Another reason is the prevalence of physical symptoms such as pain, which may be identified as organic disease. In addition, forgetfulness may lead to concern about a client having cognitive impairment or an early dementia, where in fact, as was indicated earlier, it could be a less well known symptom of depression.

Activity 7.2 Personalised practice point

Routine screening can help identify cases of depression. Simply asking the client the following during conversation is helpful:

'How have you been feeling recently?'

'Do you feel sad or tired?'

If you wanted to be more specific you may ask:

'During the last month have you been bothered by feeling down, depressed or hopeless?' and

'During the past month have you been bothered by having little interest or pleasure in doing things?'

A yes to any of these questions is considered a positive result and should be followed by the question:

'Is this something you would like help with?'

The geriatric depression scale (Yesavage et al. 1983) may be of benefit if something more formal was required as a measurement of mood. Assessment tools that help us to measure symptoms can also be used when evaluating the care plan so are useful when planning personalised care. This assessment tool was designed to be simple and not require the skills of a trained interviewer or mental health practitioner to administer. The original Geriatric Depression Scale consists of 30 questions and this may not be appropriate or possible to complete at time of assessment so a 4-item version was developed in 1994 by Katona. The 4-item geriatric scale consists of the following questions:

Are you basically satisfied with your life?	No = 1 Yes = 0
Do you feel your life is empty?	Yes = 1 No = 0
Are you afraid something bad is going to happen to you?	Yes = 1 No = 0
Do you feel happy most of the time?	Yes = 0 No = 1

Scores of more than one on the above scale are suggestive of depression and indicate the need for a more detailed assessment and possibly the need for involvement of mental health services. It is also important at this time to assess for ideas of self-harm and suicide. All clients who have ideas of suicide or self-harm should be referred to mental health services and may require an urgent assessment to provide interventions to reduce incidence of clients taking action on these thoughts. There are several ways to assess whether a client has ideas of harming themselves and many scales professionals may wish to use.

Activity 7.3   Personalised practice point

When assessing for suicidality there is little validated documented evidence to suggest that harm may be caused by being direct and asking questions such as:

'Do you ever think about ending it all?'

'Do you think that you may act on this?'

'Have you made any plans to end it all?'

'Have you ever tried to harm yourself before?'

A yes response to any of these questions should result in an assessment from the mental health team. If at all concerned when asking these questions it is worthwhile remembering that no one has ever become suicidal because they have been asked about it but people have died because they were not asked!

Care and treatment of older people with depression

Exclusion of an organic cause for the client's symptoms is paramount to planning care as many symptoms of depression can be caused by anaemia, kidney disease, liver disease and diabetes among others. Therefore an examination and full blood screen is an essential part of care planning.

Medication is often an initial intervention in the treatment of depression in older adults. This is likely because Wilson et al. (2001) identified a good evidence base that antidepressants are effective for people with moderate to severe depression. NICE (NICE/SCIE 2006) guidelines for prescribing antidepressants suggest that first line treatment should be with a selective serotonin reuptake inhibitor (SSRI). Clients' previous experiences of antidepressants along with co-morbidities and side effects should be taken into consideration when selecting an antidepressant. An antidepressant should be taken for at least four weeks before changing to another unless undesired side effects have been identified.

The following are some SSRI side effects to be mindful of:

- insomnia – poor sleep pattern and poor quality of sleep;
- agitation – active behaviour such as being unable to sit still, shouting, etc.;
- headache – pain experienced to any part of the head;
- sexual dysfunction – unable to maintain sexual relationships;
- gastrointestinal disorders – stomach upsets and associated symptoms;
- hyponatraemia – lack of salt (sodium) in the body which may also cause confusion.

Assessing levels of activity

Clients who are depressed will often feel lethargic and unmotivated. When planning care for people experiencing lethargy and low motivation it is important to help them structure their day with a mixture of meaningful activities, rest and relaxation. These activities should be individualised and interesting to the client. Identifying what the client has found stimulating and rewarding in the past will assist in achieving this. Identifying individual strengths will encourage the client to become more motivated and able to manage their mood.

Assessing personal hygiene

Encouraging clients to attend to their personal hygiene and appearance as part of their structured day is also important as neglect of self-care is very common in depressed clients and this can contribute to low self-esteem. Encouraging people to take care of their appearance can also affect their mood. This can be achieved by getting to know their personal style of clothing and grooming and ensuring that they have access to resources to help them maintain personalised care.

Assessing physical wellbeing

Regular exercise can be of benefit with depressed clients but can also be difficult to achieve due to the medical condition of this client group. Utilizing low impact exercise programmes such as extend and postural stability instruction may be an appropriate form of exercise to encourage the client to participate in. Encouraging participation in regular exercise groups therefore not only encourages supportive relationships to develop but can also improve the physical wellbeing of the client.

Assessing psychological/educational needs

Helping clients to understand their depression is good practice as clients often misunderstand their symptoms or can feel ashamed, believing it to be a sign of weakness. Giving a clear explanation of the nature of depression can frequently be an effective intervention in its own right. A common feature of depression is a tendency to be preoccupied with negative thoughts and unfounded guilt. Something that could make a difference to those who are mildly depressed who are experiencing this is to assist them to challenge these thoughts and encourage them to look at alternative interpretations. For example, perhaps a depressed woman walks out of the toilet and sees some clients laughing. Her thought is that they are laughing at her because they don't like her. What other reasons could they be laughing for?

> Maybe one had just told the other a joke.
> Maybe one had broken wind.
> Maybe a nurse had dropped something.
> Maybe the woman had toilet paper on her shoe or her dress was tucked up.
>   So, yes, they were laughing at her but not because they disliked her.

Can you think of any other interpretations?

Setting goals with the client

Goal setting is an indispensable part of helping older people with depression and for formulating a care plan. A useful way of formatting goal setting is to use the SMART mnemonic. There are many variations of this, however for the purpose of this chapter SMART will represent specific, measureable, achievable, realistic and timed. The goals should be specific and well defined. Stating you want to be a millionaire is not a goal, it is an outcome of a goal, whereas working towards a vacant promotion post is a goal and looking how that goal can be broken down further into even more specific steps will help in achieving that goal.

How will the client know they have achieved their goal?

This question is important when making the goal measurable. Identifying if the goal is within the individual's capabilities at this time, or even if the goal can be completed at all is essential when assisting the individual to make achievable goals. Can the goal be completed within the context of current availability of knowledge, resources and staff time? It is important to ascertain if the individual will manage the pressure and worry if things are not going to plan. This is the essence of making goals realistic. Time frames should be set for each stage of the goal. There should be enough time to achieve the goal but not so much time that it affects motivation to achieve that goal. Setting these parameters should prevent a state of procrastination where the client ends up more frustrated and unfocused than when the goals were first set (Lloyd 2010).

The Care Programme Approach for older people with mental health needs

The Care Programme Approach (CPA) is a way of identifying the care needs of all people with a mental illness. It provides an organised way of assessing all a person's needs if they have a mental illness and developing a single care plan which will ensure those needs are met.

The main elements of the CPA are

- a holistic assessment of the client's personal health and social care needs that identifies strengths as well as needs and encourages a recovery approach to care planning;
- a written care plan agreed in collaboration with the client and with all those involved in the delivery of an individual's care including the community mental health team, GP and carer;
- the nomination of a care coordinator who acts as the main point of contact, overseeing the delivery of the client's care, monitors for risks and arranges regular review meetings;
- ongoing and regular reviews of an individual's care plan and health and social care needs.

Personalised care planning is the point at which the service user and carer voice is best articulated. To promote recovery and independence care planning should be based on an individual's strengths as well as their needs. It should include all aspects of an individual's life where support is required, e.g. physical, social and psychological. As far as possible, mental health care services should be community based, but admission to hospital may be considered in certain circumstances. This may be if the person with mental health problems is severely disturbed and needs to be assessed in one place for their own health and safety of others (this might include those liable to be detained under the Mental Health Act 1983). Also it may not be possible to complete the assessment in the community setting if the person has complex physical and mental health problems.

The following case study and care plan (see Table 7.1) is an example of how an older person might be demonstrating signs of depression and how they could be helped through a personalised care plan.

Case study – Mrs Davies

Mrs Davies was recently admitted to hospital following a fall at home where her daughter found her. Mrs Davies is a very independent woman but feels she is not coping so well since her husband died 12 months ago. A full physical assessment indicates a broken leg and the daughter has reported a gradual weight loss over the last six months. The multidisciplinary team (MDT) and family are concerned that Mrs Davies will not be able to cope at home on her own. A care plan is needed so that Mrs Davies's mood might be improved and her confidence regained in being able to take care of herself at home. Mrs Davies would like help in developing her interests again in things that she used to enjoy so that she can spend less time alone and can develop a social network that is supportive to her independence.

The care plan can then be written from the information provided above but it is useful to put it into the APIE framework to help both the client and the practitioner clearly see what needs to be done (see Table 7.1).

Dementia

The number of people experiencing dementia is increasing and dementia is at the forefront of health policy. Person centred approaches and interventions in dementia care are expanding, making this an exciting and challenging time for dementia care and for nurses planning care for those with dementia. There are 820,00 people with dementia living in the UK (Luengo-Fernandez et al. 2010) and this number is expected to rise with the growth of the ageing population.

Table 7.1 Care plan for Mrs Davies

Assessment	Planning	Implementation	Evaluation
Mrs Davies is a 72-year-old who was admitted to hospital due to a fall. Mrs Davies has stated that she had not been looking after herself as well as she could have recently. Mrs Davies feels alone at home since the death of her husband	Mrs Davies would like to be able to walk independently within six weeks with continued support from ward staff and physiotherapy. This will improve Mrs Davies' confidence as long as motivation is maintained. From this she can set herself more goals	1 Identify activities that give pleasure and or achievement which will increase positive behaviour and motivation to do more.	Daily
		2 Work collaboratively with Mrs Davies and MDT	Weekly
		3 Identify and challenge negative automatic thoughts and record these thoughts and challenges for Mrs Davies to refer to	Daily
		4 Collaboratively make a structured plan for each day including activities of enjoyment as well as necessary tasks	Weekly
		5 Medication and medical situation review with medical staff as this can influence progress	Weekly
		6 Monitor and review progress through set goal and adapt as needed	Monthly

The ICD-10 Classification of Mental and Behavioural Disorders (World Health Organisation 2010) defines dementia as:

> A syndrome due to disease of the brain, usually of a chronic or progressive nature, in which there is disturbance of multiple higher cortical functions, including memory, thinking, orientation, comprehension, calculation, learning capacity, language, and judgement. Consciousness is not clouded. The impairments of cognitive function are commonly accompanied, and occasionally preceded by deterioration in emotional control, social behaviour or motivation.
>
> (WHO 2010)

Activity 7.4 Critical reflection

When a person has a diagnosis of dementia, what signs and symptoms would you expect to observe in the person and how might they affect the person?

The stages of dementia

The World Health Organisation (1992) provides comprehensive information on the stages of dementia and the general signs and symptoms. These are briefly outlined below.

Mild dementia

Decline in cognitive abilities causes impaired performance in daily living, but not to a degree that makes the individual dependent on others. More complicated daily tasks or recreational activities cannot be undertaken. There is a loss of short-term memory which can be accompanied by confusion, poor judgement and unwillingness to make decisions. The person might also experience anxiety, agitation or distress over perceived changes, and inability to manage everyday tasks.

Moderate dementia

Decline in cognitive abilities makes the individual unable to function without the assistance of another in daily living, including shopping and handling money. In the home, only simple chores are preserved. Activities are increasingly restricted and poorly sustained. More support is required, including reminders to eat, wash, dress and void. The person might become increasingly forgetful and may fail to recognise people. Distress, aggression and anger are not uncommon, perhaps due to frustration. Risks may include wandering and getting lost, leaving taps running or forgetting to light the gas. The person may behave inappropriately, for example, leaving home in night clothes. They may also experience hallucinations.

Severe dementia

Decline in cognitive abilities is characterised by an absence, or virtual absence, of being able to form their own opinions and ideas. There may be an inability to recognise familiar objects, surroundings or people, but there may be some flashes of recognition. The person may become increasingly frail physically. The person may also start to shuffle or walk unsteadily, eventually becoming confined to bed or a wheelchair. There may be difficulty eating and sometimes swallowing, a general loss of interest in food, weight loss, incontinence and a gradual loss of speech.

Palliative care was not always considered as being important in dementia care but more recently has become recognised as an unidentified need and therefore should be incorporated into care from the time of diagnosis until death (NICE/SCIE 2006).

Activity 7.5   Critical reflection: defining dementia

We often use the word dementia as a diagnosis, which in fact it is not. Dementia is used as a term to cover all disorders of the brain that are 'organic', which means changes to the structure of the brain take place. Before reading the next section spend a few moments reflecting upon your knowledge of what the different types of dementia are and how their symptoms vary.

Understanding dementia

Dementia is often used as an umbrella term to define a group of syndromes characterised by a progressive decline in cognition which is of sufficient severity to interfere eventually with most activities of living, ultimately leading to death. Alzheimer's disease, vascular dementia and dementia with Lewy bodies are the most common types. The National Audit Office (2007) suggests the following can be observed:

- Alzheimer's disease accounts for 62 per cent of dementias in the UK. The pathology alters chemistry and structure of the brain, causing cells to die.
- Dementia is caused by problems with the supply of oxygen to the brain. Strokes and disease of the small blood vessels related to conditions such as hypertension can cause this. Vascular dementia and mixed vascular with Alzheimer's dementias make up approximately 30 per cent of dementias.
- Dementia with Lewy bodies is caused by protein deposits inside nerve cells in the brain, which interrupt its normal function. It shares symptoms with Parkinson's disease, including slowness of movement.

The term 'personhood' refers to the state or condition of being an individual, and in dementia this is seen to diminish as the disease progresses. It is important that personhood is maintained in dementia by recognizing and respecting the identity of the person. Kitwood (1997) suggests that personhood is very important in older people's mental health care and is often ignored or marginalised as the person becomes known by their diagonisis only. He argues that the behaviours of staff and society contribute to this marginalization process as people become recognised by their unsociable behaviours and are even labelled as 'naughty', 'manipulative' and 'aggressive' when they may simply be trying to get our attention in order to recognise their needs. In developing person centered care plans we must therefore be able to demonstrate and understand the personal or individual nature of the care plan in meeting a person's needs.

While dementia itself is not a diagnostic term it is used to describe the many symptoms a person may experience when suffering from the different types of dementia. Each person is different, and the way a person reacts to their dementia will be shaped by their personality and personal history. Dementia is caused by damage to the brain which gets worse over time. People with dementia are dealing with a disability that is hidden from view: this is confusing and difficult for the person with dementia and those around them and can put up a barrier to getting to know the person. If you understand the most common difficulties that people with dementia struggle with, you will be better able to understand the person you want to get to know.

> We feel as if we are hanging onto a high cliff, above a lurking black hole. Daily tasks are complex. Nothing is automatic anymore. Everything is as if we are first learning.
>
> (Bryden 2005: 98)

Care planning for dementia

The Dementia UK report (Alzheimer's Society 2007) stated that the UK's health and social care system is characterised by a widespread failure to support people with dementia and their families. The National Dementia Strategy for England (DH 2009) aims to provide a more standardised approach to care and focuses on three key areas: improved awareness, earlier diagnosis and intervention, and a higher quality of care. The aims stated in this document include

- raise awareness and understanding of dementia;
- earlier diagnosis and clearer care pathways for clients with dementia;
- improvement in the quality of care for clients with dementia.

The National Institute for Health and Clinical Excellence (NICE) together with the Social Care Institute for Excellence (SCIE) has published quality standards for dementia that describe what a high standard of care should look like (NICE/SCIE 2006). It recommends that all people with dementia have an assessment and an ongoing personalised care plan that identifies a named care coordinator and addresses their individual needs. The care plan should ensure the right treatment is identified for the individual's personal needs. It also helps to assess what care is needed and how it will be provided.

In dementia care therefore the holistic assessment is important to the development of a care plan. There will be changing needs to be identified as the disease progresses and ongoing review of the care plan is vital. The effects of dementia can be very distressing for the person concerned and their family and friends. It can cause changes in character and behaviour, as well as affecting memory, speech and understanding. The care plan should ensure quality of life throughout the dementia journey and be person centred. Early diagnosis enables the planning of care throughout the journey reflecting the need of the person with dementia. The diagnosis of dementia demands a broad range of skills and relies on accurate clinical evidence gained through personal history, medical examination and investigation of the person (Burns and Hope 1997).

Activity 7.6   Critical reflection

What assessments could be used to help identify the person's cognitive ability and functional skills?

Life story work is an individual approach to understand the person with dementia and assist in identifying the person's life experiences and help inform care planning. Life story work enhances person centred care by allowing nurses to make the link between past and present (McKeown et al. 2010). The Royal College of Nursing and the Alzheimer's Society have also produced a document that is free to order/download called 'This is Me' which allows people who know the client to record their personal preferences and requirements (Alzheimer's Society 2010). The following case study and care plan (Table 7.2) provide an example of how care could be organised in a way that encourages everyone to contribute to a person centred care plan.

Case study – Mrs Jones

Mrs Jones was referred by her GP to the memory service for further assessment of cognitive functioning with a view to diagnosis and treatment options. Mrs Jones was diagnosed with Alzheimer's type dementia and commenced cholinesterase inhibitors. She lives alone and has been managing independently at home but her daughter had expressed concern about her compliance with medication, her cooking/shopping skills and how she was managing her personal care. Her daughter also expressed concern that her mother was isolating herself at home. Mrs Jones agreed that the home situation had become more difficult to manage since her memory had declined and discussed how she wanted to maintain her independence at home. She agreed to further support at home to help maintain skills but did not wish for ongoing support from carers at present.

Delirium

Delirium is an important problem especially in older medical clients. Delirium (sometimes called 'acute confusional state') is a common clinical syndrome characterised by disturbed consciousness, cognitive function or perception, which has an acute onset and fluctuating course. It is a serious condition that is associated with poor outcomes as suggested by Young and Inouye (2007). However, it can be prevented and treated if dealt with urgently. Eleven to 42 per cent of elderly clients have delirium when admitted to hospital (Siddiqi et al. 2006); elderly

Table 7.2 Care plan for Mrs Jones

Assessment	Planning	Implementation	Evaluation
1 Poor compliancy of medication – Mrs Jones forgets to take her morning tablets	1 Improve compliancy – Mrs Jones is to take her medication regularly as prescribed	1 Arrange review of medication by GP/pharmacist 2 Arrange to visit Mrs Jones and assess how she manages her medication presently 3 Encourage use of prompts/routine – use of calendar/note pad to mark when tablets are taken – positioning of tablets 4 Arrange vena link/telecare tablet dispenser if appropriate 5 Arrange regular visits for one week at morning times to prompt Mrs Jones and review routine	Weekly
2 Mrs Jones has been neglecting her diet at home resulting in some weight loss	1 Maintain adequate diet 2 Maintain weight 3 Mrs Jones to continue to manage meal preparation	1 Record weight 2 Arrange referral to Occupational Therapy for kitchen assessment 3 Arrange visit with Mrs Jones and discuss management of meals – likes/dislikes – shopping plan	Weekly
3 Mrs Jones has become isolated at home – she expressed how she has lost confidence in going out on her own and has reduced social contacts	1 Improve confidence and increase social stimulation	1 Engage with Mrs Jones re previous activities in the community and aim to re-establish 2 Use of Life Story Work 3 Introduction to organizations if appropriate to aid memory – healthy living projects, memory café	Monthly

(Continued)

Table 7.2 *(Continued)*

Assessment	Planning	Implementation	Evaluation
4 Diagnosis of Alzheimer's type dementia – resulting in a trial of cholinesterase inhibitors – Aricept/Donepezil	1 Improve or stabilise cognition and functional abilities 2 Slow the rate of decline of cognition and functioning abilities 3 Ongoing assessment of benefits of medication as per NICE/SCIE guidelines	1 Explanation of diagnosis to the client and family and information regarding the medication/diagnosis 2 Baseline assessments to be completed as a measure for benefits 3 Review of client's medication – any interactions/contra-indications 4 Inform client of side effects and management of same 5 Explain to client regarding titration of medication and review by memory team 6 Ensure contact numbers are made available to client and family/carer	Monthly

people who are hospitalised have a 50 per cent greater risk of developing delirium. Clients who develop delirium have high mortality, institutionalization and complication rates, and have longer lengths of stay in hospital than non-delirious clients. (Marcantonio et al. 2005).

Clients are at high risk if they have the following predisposing risk factors:

- older persons (>65 yrs);
- known dementia (some will also have an intercurrent delirium);
- cognitive impairment – screen using AMT or MMSE – (if positive on screening, some will have a delirium);
- severe physical or mental health disorders;
- polypharmacy (more than four drugs);
- fracture of neck of femur;
- visual and hearing impairment.

Assessment of delirium

Social and cultural needs

Families are a very important source of information as they know what the person is usually like, and may notice slight changes early on. Gaining a history from relatives, carers or close friends is an essential part of the assessment process. Many polices around older people's care suggests that families should be involved in care planning especially when the person is unable to speak for themselves.

Physical health care needs

It is common for there to be a disturbance in sleepwake cycle. The person can develop insomnia and often be restless at night. Daytime drowsiness can be seen. Symptoms are often worse at night. Poor sleep patterns can have a direct influence upon diet and exercise as opportunities to maintain physical health during the day are often missed due to excessive sleeping during the day.

Psychological needs

Consciousness and attention may be impaired. There is reduced ability to direct, focus, sustain and shift attention. Cognition or thought processes are generally globally impaired. There is impairment of immediate recall and recent memory but relatively generally intact remote memory. The person will often be disorientated in time and place and experience impairment in abstract thinking and comprehension. The person can develop hallucinations which in the main are visual. Paranoid delusions are also common, i.e. feelings of being poisoned. The person will often experience emotional disturbances and these may fluctuate from one emotion to another many times during the course of a day. These emotional disturbances include depression, anxiety/fear, irritability/aggression, euphoria, apathy and wondering perplexity.

Levels of activity

The client may experience over or under activity from their norm and there may be unpredictable shifts from one to the other. Along with this there may also be an increased or decreased flow of speech. Increased agitation can lead to restlessness and wandering which in turn increases the risk of falls and fractures. It may be necessary to carry out a full risk assessment to help the person cope with such risks in a positive and safe way, e.g. using bed rails at night and providing support or walking aids when walking around. Physical activity is important for the overall wellbeing of the older person and while they may not be as active as they have been in the past, ensuring regular exercise helps the person to remain as healthy as possible.

A good history supplemented by a reliable screening instrument such as the Confusion Assessment Method (CAM) is currently the most effective way of detecting delirium (Gonzalez et al. 2004). Clinical observation utilizing the Delirium Index (DI) in conjunction with the Mini-Mental State Examination (MMSE) is considered to be the most effective way of monitoring the person's progress (Peck 2005).

Activity 7.7   Critical reflection

Why do you think it is important to watch out for delirium? Make a list of your answers before reading the next section.

Clients who are delirious are unable to participate in their own care. They may pull out IV lines (drips) or remove necessary oxygen tubes or other treatments. They are at a very high risk of falling and often resistant to offers of help to prevent this. Can you think of any other reasons identification is important?

The importance of identifying onset of symptoms in delirium

- The identification of delirium can be made in contrast to dementia where the cognitive impairment has been present and progressive over at least six months typically. This is again why gaining a history of current presentation is important.
- A sudden onset – over minutes – is more suggestive of an acute vascular episode such as a stroke or heart attack rather than delirium.
- An onset over a few days is suggestive of an infection or being haemodynamically unstable. Blood tests are important to rule out any problems in the functioning of different organs or systems within the body.
- An onset over a week or two might be secondary to heart failure or polypharmacy. Further investigations will be required to rule out these causes.
- A sub-acute onset of a month or more is rarely seen but can occur, e.g. in sub-acute bacterial endocarditis (infection of the heart).

The World Health Organisation International Classification of Diseases (ICD-10) (WHO 2007) diagnosis of delirium is outlined below:

- impaired attention which can also indicate a clouding of consciousness;
- disturbance of cognition including memory of recent events and disorientation in time or place;
- psychomotor disturbance, e.g. hyperactivity or hypo-activity;
- disturbance of sleep, e.g. symptoms worse at night;
- recent/rapid onset with diurnal variation;
- objective evidence from history from an informant, abnormalities O/E or in investigations of a cause for the delirium;
- visual hallucinations and paranoid delusions are also typical.

The signs of delirium

- **Being less aware of what is going on around you** The environment may become an unfamiliar place to the person and familiar faces could become distorted. Agitation can occur as the person becomes afraid of such unfamiliarity and families or carers can become distressed when they cannot help the person recognise familiar things.

- **An inability to pay attention, feeling agitated and restless and unable to sit still or wanting to wander** The person may feel the need to move around in order to cope with the agitation and restlessness and should be encouraged to take exercise unless there is a risk of falls. If so the care plan will need to identify that the person should be supported when walking around.
- **Being less aware of where you are or what you are doing there** A person may not only be unable to recognise familiar places but may also suffer from short term memory loss. However long term memory remains intact. Helping a person to remember using objects such as calendars, diaries and watches may alleviate some of this distress.
- **Decreased short-term memory indicates that the person is not only distressed but that they may also be disorientated** Imagine driving in the fog or walking around in the dark – without familiar landmarks we can quickly become confused and distressed. Such distress naturally affects our ability to store and retrieve memories and information.
- **Seeing and talking to people or things that are not there** This can be caused by perceptual disturbances in the brain. As the brain interprets everything that we see anything that affects the regular functioning of the brain also affects our interpretation of events. We only need to think of the effects of alcohol or recreational drugs to imagine how this might feel. However if perceptual disturbance lasts for a longer period of time or upon waking it can be very distressing and can affect the person's quality of sleep and rest.
- **Mood changes such as anxiousness, irritability or depression** These are often evident in a person suffering from delirium as they try to make sense of their situation. A sudden onset can be particularly distressing and people may become aggressive or withdrawn as they try to cope with feelings of fear and threat.
- **Sleeping during the day but waking up at night** This can also become a problem for the person who is experiencing delirium and can cause disturbance not only to their mood and sleep patterns but also to their diet, exercise and social activities. There may be many reasons sleep patterns become disturbed and this will need to be assessed on an individual basis.

There are many causes of delirium. Some of these include:

- infections – such as urinary or chest;
- conditions which limit oxygen to the brain
- alcohol or drug intoxication, or suddenly stopping alcohol;
- changes in body fluid level such as dehydration;

- abnormal blood glucose levels;
- reactions to medicines such as sleeping pills or pain medications;
- recent surgery;
- severe pain;
- having a high temperature;
- constipation;
- infarction causing restricted blood supply to the heart;
- intracranial event, e.g. trauma, stroke, encephalitis, meningitis causing restricted blood supply to the brain.

Treatment of delirium

To treat the delirium there is a need to identify and then treat the cause. Despite blood tests, x-rays or other tests to find out the most likely cause, it is possible that a cause may not be identified. There should be a multidisciplinary approach towards the treatment with all disciplines having input. Assessment and management of pain or other discomfort is an important part of the treatment. Quite often delirium has more than one cause and therefore all must be treated to resolve the problem. While upsetting for family and friends, it is not advised to give medication such as sedatives to clients with delirium unless they pose a risk to themselves or others. The care plan shown in Table 7.3 provides an example of how a person

Table 7.3 Care plan for Mr Evans

Assessment	Planning	Implementation	Evaluation
Mr Evans has become increasingly agitated and has been both verbally and physically aggressive at times	To minimise any accidental harm to self or any harm to others To provide a safe environment for all To alleviate episodes of distressed behaviour and to reduce the incidence of this	1 Ensure the safety of other clients and the environment 2 Give Mr Evans space – with minimum number of staff 3 Get Mr Evans' attention before speaking/say one thing at a time/do not argue 4 Acknowledge Mr Evans' distress/be aware of your body language 5 Give rational explanations for the situation 6 Ensure all physical investigations have been carried out 7 Consider the use of pharmacological intervention as a last resort following NICE guidelines and using lowest possible doses	Daily

suffering from delirium can be cared for. Mr Evans has been admitted to hospital for investigations following a referral from his GP. He complains of feeling confused and disorientated even in familiar surroundings.

Conclusion

This chapter has outlined three main areas of practice where the student might find themselves. Care planning for people who are experiencing depression, dementia or delirium in older life should always be focused upon the individual needs of the client and their care planned appropriately. This chapter has outlined some of the needs older people suffering from mental health problems might express. It is very important to bear in mind that personalised care for older people is based upon good communication and assessment skills so that appropriate goals and interventions can be put into place. This might require the student to expand their communication skills so that they are able to act on behalf of and in the best interests of clients in their care and within the multidisciplinary and inter-professional team. Working with families and carers is particularly important in gaining accurate information so that appropriate personalised care plans can be put in place as soon as possible.

References

Alzheimer's Society (2007) *Dementia UK: The Full Report*. http://alzheimers.org.uk/site/scripts/download-info.php?fileID=2 (accessed 10 February 2012).

Alzheimer's Society (2010) *This is Me*. Free to download at http://alzheimers.org.uk/site/scripts/download_info.php?fileID=849 (accessed 10 February 2012).

Bryden, C. (2005) *Dancing with Dementia*. London: Jessica Kingsley.

Burns, A. and Hope, T. (1997) Clinical aspects of the dementias of old age. In R. Jacoby and C. Oppenheimer (eds) *Psychiatry in the Elderly*, 2nd edn. Oxford: Oxford University Press, pp. 456–93.

Craig, R. and Mindell, J. (2007) *Health Survey for England 2005*. Leeds: The Information Centre.

DH (Department of Health) (2001) *National Serivce Framework for Older People*. London: HMSO.

DH (2009) *Living Well with Dementia: A National Dementia Strategy*. London: The Stationery Office.

Gonzalez, M., DePablo, D.J., Fuente, E. et al. (2004) Instrument for detection of delirium in general hospitals: adaptation of the confusion assessment method. *Psychosomatics*, 45: 426–31.

Katona, C.L.E. (1994) *Depression in Old Age*. Chichester: John Wiley & Sons.

Kitwood, T. (1997) *Dementia Reconsidered: The Person Comes First*. Buckingham: Open University Press.

Lloyd, M. (2010) *A Practical Guide to Care Planning in Health and Social Care.* Maidenhead: Open University Press.

Luengo-Fernandez, R., Leal, J. and Gray, A. (2010) *Dementia 2010: The Prevalence, Economic Cost and Research Funding of Dementia Compared with Other Major Diseases.* http://www.dementia2010.org/reports/Dementia2010full.pdf (accessed 10 February 2012).

Marcantonio, E.R., Kiely, D.K., Simon, S.E. et al. (2005) Outcomes of older people admitted to postacute facilities with delirium. *Journal of the American Geriatrics Society*, 53(6): 963–9.

McKeown, J., Clarke, A., Ingleton, C., Ryan, T. and Repper, J. (2010) The use of life story work with people with dementia to enhance person-centred care. *International Journal of Older People Nursing*, 5(2): 148–58.

National Audit Office (2007) *Improving Services and Support for People with Dementia.* London: The Stationery Office.

NICE/SCIE (2006) *Dementia: Supporting People with Dementia and their Carers in Health and Social Care.* Clinical Guideline 42. London: National Institute for Health and Clinical Excellence.

Office of National Statistics (2009) Life expectancy at birth and at age 65 by local areas in the United Kingdom, 2006–08. *Statistical Bulletin*, 21.

Peck, S. (2005) *Clinical Guideline for the Care and Treatment of Older People with Dementia in a General Hospital Setting*, 2nd edn. Isle of Wight Healthcare NHS Trust. http://www.iow.nhs.uk/uploads/Mental/Older/Dementia%20Guideline.pdf (accessed 10 February 2012).

Siddiqi, N., House, A.O. and Holmes, J.D. (2006) Occurrence and outcome of delirium in medical in-patients: a systematic literature review. *Age and Ageing*, 35: 350–64.

Wilson, K., Mottram, P., Sivanranthan, A. et al. (2001) Antidepressant versus placebo for depressed elderly. *Cochrane Library*, issue 4. Oxford: Update Software.

World Health Organisation (1992) *The ICD-10 Classification of Mental and Behavioural Disorders Diagnostic Criteria for Research.* Geneva: WHO.

World Health Organisation (2010) *International Statistical Classification of Diseases and Related Health Problems*, 10th revision. http://apps.who.int/classifications/icd10browse2010/en (accessed 10 February 2010).

Yesavage, J., Brink, T.L., Rose, T. et al. (1983) Development and validation of a geriatric depression screening scale: a preliminary report. *Journal of Psychiatric Research*, 17: 37–49.

Young, J. and Inouye, S.K. (2007) Delirium in older people. *British Medical Journal*, 334(7598): 843–6.

8 Conclusion

Marjorie Lloyd

Personalised care planning in mental health care may appear to be a new concept but in fact it has been around since at least the 1980s. When health and social care began moving into the community, policy and service providers recognised that community care would only be successful if people were more involved in their care and if care services recognised the diverse needs of individual people and their local communities and cultures. People who lived in highly populated and industrial areas were more likely to have different health and social care needs to those who lived in rural isolated cultures. Other issues such as employment, education and family support and resilience were also identified as being of great influence upon the health and social care of the populations.

The personalisation agenda in more recent health and social care policy has continued to embed diversity and resilience within society so that people are more able to self-care or self-manage their individual needs. Such empowering practices not only encourage people to be less dependent upon health and social care services but also reduce dependency upon the state to support people over what can be a long period of time, particularly in long term conditions such as mental illness.

Chapter 2 on mental health in primary care and Chapter 6 on mental health care for people with learning disabilities provide an interesting overview of how such polices have changed. During this time people who have learning disabilities are now living entirely in their own homes with varying levels of support but hospital care is largely a service of the past that is no longer needed or required. People with learning disabilities do however provide a good example of how services can change towards a more personalised agenda that works best when the person in need is at the centre of the care plan. Similarly, primary care services have expanded considerably in order to reflect a recovery approach to health and social care in supporting people within a local community to live as independent lives as possible.

The World Health Organisation (WHO) spend much of their time and money on helping different countries improve their health and social care profile and collect and share information from across the world. In October 2011 they produced the following 10 facts about mental health that they found during the course of their evaluation studies (see WHO 2011):

1   About half of mental disorders begin before the age of 14. Around 20 per cent of the world's children and adolescents are estimated to have mental disorders or problems, with similar types of disorders being reported across cultures. Yet, regions of the world with the highest percentage of

population under the age of 19 have the poorest level of mental health resources. Most low- and middle-income countries have only one child psychiatrist for every 1 to 4 million people.

2 Depression is characterised by sustained sadness and loss of interest along with psychological, behavioural and physical symptoms. It is ranked as the leading cause of disability worldwide.

3 On average about 800,000 people commit suicide every year, 86 per cent of them in low- and middle-income countries. More than half of the people who kill themselves are aged between 15 and 44. The highest suicide rates are found among men in eastern European countries. Mental disorders are one of the most prominent and treatable causes of suicide.

4 War and other major disasters have a large impact on mental health and psychosocial wellbeing. Rates of mental disorder tend to double after emergencies.

5 Mental disorders are among the risk factors for communicable and non-communicable diseases. They can also contribute to unintentional and intentional injury.

6 Stigma about mental disorders and discrimination against patients and families prevent people from seeking mental health care. In South Africa, a public survey showed that most people thought mental illnesses were related to either stress or a lack of willpower rather than to medical disorders. Contrary to expectations, levels of stigma were higher in urban areas and among people with higher levels of education.

7 Human rights violations of psychiatric patients are routinely reported in most countries. These include physical restraint, seclusion and denial of basic needs and privacy. Few countries have a legal framework that adequately protects the rights of people with mental disorders.

8 There is huge inequity in the distribution of skilled human resources for mental health across the world. Shortages of psychiatrists, psychiatric nurses, psychologists and social workers are among the main barriers to providing treatment and care in low- and middle-income countries. Low-income countries have 0.05 psychiatrists and 0.42 nurses per 100,000 people. The rate of psychiatrists in high income countries is 170 times greater and for nurses is 70 times greater.

9 In order to increase the availability of mental health services, there are five key barriers that need to be overcome: the absence of mental health from the public health agenda and the implications for funding; the current organization of mental health services; lack of integration within primary care; inadequate human resources for mental health; and lack of public mental health leadership.

10 Governments, donors and groups representing mental health workers, patients and their families need to work together to increase mental health services, especially in low- and middle-income countries. The financial resources needed are relatively modest: US$ 2 per person per year in low-income countries and US$ 3-4 in lower middle-income countries.

While the above facts are based on the world population and this book has been written by people in the UK, there are still many similarities to be found across the world that could improve mental health provision and care planning, if only the resources were available. Unfortunately many of the issues facing the world of mental health care cannot be addressed in this book but can be read and accessed from the World Health Organisation's Website, where more specific mental health sections are available (http://www.who.int/en/).

What is of concern is fact number 8 – the absence of mental health from the public health agenda and the implications for funding; the current organization of mental health services; lack of integration within primary care; inadequate human resources for mental health; and lack of public mental health leadership. These are all things that can be incorporated into the personalised mental health care planning agenda and can provide proof or evidence for empowering care planning practice. In Chapter 2 there is evidence that mental health problems can be addressed in primary care using a personalised care planning process. We would however benefit from working more inter-professionally between primary mental health care services and secondary care services such as hospitals and community mental health teams. Team working is something that perhaps everyone in mental health care service now takes for granted but may need to be developed further. Chapter 4 on care planning in acute care identifies the importance of team working for effective mental health care planning. The demand for collaborative and inter-professional practice is perhaps a legacy of the changes in mental health policy and practice.

Developing a recovery focused approach to mental health care provision or even reorganizing mental health services to accommodate the recovery approach better could also be developed from the ground floor of practice where person-alised care planning actually takes place. If we truly believe and hope for a more personalised mental health care planning system then we should be involving clients more in developing their care package that is unique to their individual needs. In Chapter 3, care planning in the community mental health team gives some anecdotal evidence or stories about the reality of practice and how different it can be from what one might expect. Dealing with bureaucratic systems on behalf of clients can take up a great deal of the practitioner's time. However if that is what the client needs at that time identified by them then working in a personalised way that is what they should get. Many practitioners may think that it is not their job to sort out domestic issues but we know and the WHO facts above support the notion that any psychological trauma that causes stress can also lead to loss of quality of life, work, homes and individual lives if not addressed. Listening to such stories therefore reminds us that personalised mental health care planning is always about individual needs and not about what the service can offer someone. The obvious example is the fantastically beautiful, carefully worded care plan that appears to have ticked all the boxes in providing evidence based practice. This may be so but the practitioner has to ask themselves, is this something that we can realistically provide and more importantly, is it what the client needs?

Working in a recovery focused way to provide personalised mental health services requires us to question how and why we have or have not involved a client in their care planning. Chapter 1 provides an overview of this process with some examples. However in mental health care we cannot ignore that fact that much of our work involves managing risk and developing our knowledge of laws and policies to help the client to get the best out of the service. An empowerment model may not always appear to be the most appropriate model in circumstances where the person may be confused, acutely unwell, at risk of harming themselves or others or simply neglecting their everyday basic needs. On the contrary, an empowerment model is precisely what is needed in these circumstances to help both the person and practitioner see what is trying to be achieved, which is to help the person back to their normal levels of functioning as quickly as possible. An empowerment model therefore encompasses a recovery approach to mental health care that enables us to keep the client at the centre of the care plan at all times.

Yet still we hear of people not being listened to in ombudsman reports into older people's care and quality commissioning reports into mental health care. Recent reports found that worryingly less than 50 per cent of people felt fully involved in their care plan. The Care Quality Commission (CQC 2010) has published its report on improving mental health care provision which includes the following five points. These are all vital in providing quality care.

1   Making sure that care is centred on people's needs and protects their rights
2   Championing joined-up care
3   Acting swiftly to help eliminate poor quality care
4   Promoting high quality care
5   Regulating effectively, in partnership

(CQC 2010: 3)

Much of what is identified above can also be found in the personalised care plans in this book across the service spectrum. However the care plans may not be so elaborate as to fail or so vague as to be misleading. The value of a good care plan is therefore simply in its ability to identify and address individual needs. When the CQC (2010) asked service users and carers what they thought were important to improve practice they were told to:

- Build on what was good before, use existing groups and networks and keep the user voice broad based and real.
- Include people from the start of the process and involve them in everything we do at all levels.
- Put involvement at the heart of any strategy – dedicated resources must be made available to enable meaningful engagement.
- Model best practice in a way that is recognised by providers.
- Employing people with mental health problems is fundamental – to consider becoming a MINDFUL EMPLOYER®, an initiative aimed at increasing

awareness of mental health at work and providing support for businesses in recruiting and retaining staff with mental health needs.

- Partnership working and co-production – including starting with an initial approach to our work on mental health for the next two to three years but co-produce the medium/longer term plan with service users and carers.
- Subject all products to service user and carer impact assessments and build in user focused evaluation of the action plan.
- Reflect views from the consultation process.
- Use a range of mechanisms for achieving involvement and identify separate mechanisms for considering different perspectives.
- Help improve contact with mental health service users and carers through LINKs.
- CQC should have sound standards and should check the quality of involvement.

(CQC 2010: 8)

Whatever the future for mental health care it is likely that people will need a care plan of some sort. Furthermore with developing societies increasing rather than reducing the stress levels that people already feel themselves under there is more likely to be a higher not lower demand for effective and efficient mental health care provision. The care plan can be the central point therefore in which all other mental health services can grow and develop. In keeping person centred care at the heart of care planning we are not only ensuring that personalised care planning can flourish but we are also identifying what it is that is important to individual people, practitioners and service providers.

The development of mental health services has provided us with the opportunity to move away from surveillance based practice that is focused upon risk and dependence towards a more empowering and emancipatory service. Such a vision would keep personalised and recovery focused care on the agenda of every multidisciplinary team meeting, every policy that is developed and every lecture or conference that is presented on mental health services.

References

Care Quality Commission (2010) *Position Statement and Action Plan for Mental Health 2010–2015*. London: CQC.

World Health Organisation (2011) *10 Facts on Mental Health*. Geneva: WHO. http://www.who.int/features/factfiles/mental_health/mental_health_facts/en/index8.html (accessed 8 February 2012).

Appendix: Mental State Examination (MSE)

The MSE (adapted from Singh and Kirkby 2001) has been developed over time to provide a full medical picture of the person's problems. It does not include many social areas of a person's life but it could be argued that these needs will become apparent when assessing someone's thoughts and behaviour.

For example, a person who is suspicious of others may not want to mix with them or may neglect themselves because they have no reason to look after themselves. The following list is therefore what is generally considered to be a full assessment of someone's mental health and can indicate both relapse and recovery if carried out over time.

The person who is doing the assessing should be sensitive to the client's needs and abilities during the assessment and not cause unnecessary stress in trying to complete the MSE. It may therefore require a number of meetings rather than just one.

Overview of the MSE

1 **Appearance and behaviour** You may need the help of other people to give information upon whether this has changed recently, for example has the person become less careful about their hair, and bathing? Are their clothes clean, do their nails need cutting or are their skin and hair dull and unwashed? It is important to get an individualised picture of how the person usually prefers to look and dress. In addition how has their behaviour changed if at all over the last few weeks? This is also a good opportunity to find out about personalised routines, e.g. time of going to bed/getting up/eating, etc.

2 **Speech** You will need to observe their speech pattern while discussing their needs to see if it appears to be unusually fast or slow. Again you will need to find out how this has changed over the last few weeks. Is the person usually quite loud or talkative or are they usually very quiet and slow when talking? As well as the rate of speech you can observe other aspects of speech including slurring, dribbling, strength of voice and emotion, which can all indicate many different causes that will need exploring further.

3 **Mood and affect** can be difficult to assess because you are asking people to talk about how they feel and they may not be familiar with talking about their feelings. A rating scale is useful here, e.g. 1–10, but you must identify the parameters, e.g. 1 = very sad and 10 = very happy. Be careful not to use words that people may not understand, e.g. 'labile' and try to use everyday words that people will be familiar with, e.g. irritable, angry, tired, etc. This can also help to avoid confusion and makes writing out the care plan much easier. Pictures of happy/sad faces may also be used on a scale so that people can point to these, rather than having to put into words how they are feeling.

4 **Form of thought** This is where you are trying to find out if a person's thoughts are racing or intrusive (cannot switch off) and how thoughts are affecting the individual's behaviour, e.g. cannot concentrate. Do they feel like someone can read their thoughts or hear them out loud, or as if someone is even putting words into their head (thought insertion)? Are their thoughts all mixed up and do they have difficulty expressing their thoughts coherently (word salad)? It is important to pinpoint exactly how the person's thoughts are affecting their behaviour.

5 **Content of thought** includes what the person expresses rather than how they form their thoughts as identified above. This can include some very frightening material so may be difficult to express, particularly in suicidality. However it is important to help the person express the content of their thoughts using all of your communication and interpersonal skills so that the correct help can be offered. People may tell you that they have strange beliefs (delusions) or behaviours (obsessions and rituals) or that they feel that they are going to die. Often it is a person trying to make sense of what is happening to them that may lead to such content of thought, so it is very important to discuss without being dismissive or patronizing. Their fears are very real to them.

6 **Perception** Similar to thought content and form perception helps us to identify how the person sees what is happening to them so is important to use good communication skills. You might ask the person to tell you a story as way of identifying symptoms such as persecution (thinks people are out to get them); hallucinations (seeing things that are not there); depersonalisation (not feeling like a real person); or derealization (feeling like they are not in the real world). Perceptual disturbances can occur for all sorts of reasons (including physical illness and infection) and can include all five senses of hearing, seeing, touch, taste and smell.

7 **Cognition** This indicates how the brain is acting in response to the person's situation and this can include many signs that are subtle and difficult to identify unless you have experience and knowledge of how the brain works. For example, does the person appear to be sleepy or drowsy, are they able to communicate with you well and coherently? Do they have

problems remembering things in the short term and/or the long term and are they able to tell you where they are (orientation)? Some simple tests to assess cognition include counting backwards in series of seven or asking people what day it is and their date of birth. More complicated tests may be required if this is an area that is difficult to assess including psychological and physical testing, e.g. CT scan.

8 **Insight** This can be a difficult area to assess because essentially it is about whether you agree with one another. Assessing insight therefore requires many skills in questioning and communication and can develop into a full blown counselling session if not careful. The point of this part of the examination is to assess how much the person knows about what they are experiencing and their understanding of their symptoms and behaviour. This is important when trying to involve people in their care plan so that you are able to agree upon what needs to be done. Sometimes if this presents too much of a risk then mental health law may need to be used to ensure that everyone feels safe during this stage of assessment.

Reference

Singh, B. and Kirkby, A. (2001) The psychiatric interview: the mental state examination and formulation. In S. Bloch and B. Singh (eds) *Foundations of Clnical Psychiatry*. Melbourne: Melbourne University.

Index